Mastering AI Web Development with Replit

Build Your Own Intelligent Websites

By

Dr. Hesham Mohamed Elsherif

About the Author

Dr. Hesham Mohamed Elsherif stands at the forefront of library management, research, and the practical implementation of Artificial Intelligence (AI) in educational and library systems. With over 22 years of dedicated service in the field, he brings a wealth of expertise that bridges the worlds of technology, organizational leadership, and scholarship.

Dr. Elsherif's academic credentials are as diverse as they are impressive. He holds two doctoral degrees - one in **Management and Organizational Leadership** and the other in **Information Systems and Technology**. This dual specialization has equipped him with a holistic perspective on how institutions can effectively integrate emerging technologies, particularly AI, to optimize resourc allocation, streamline operational processes, and enrich learning experiences.

A recognized authority in **empirical research methodology**, Dr. Elsherif specializes in **qualitative approaches** and **action research**. His mastery of these methodologies has not only bolstered his own scholarly work but has also allowed him to pioneer new ways of investigating and implementing AI-driven solutions in school, academic, and public libraries. Whether he is designing user-centric AI tools or conducting in-depth studies on technology adoption, Dr. Elsherif's methodical and data-driven approach consistently yields impactful, real-world results.

Over the years, he has made significant strides in shaping the academic community - not just as a **professional researcher**, but also as an **Adjunct Professor**. In the classroom, Dr. Elsherif has a remarkable ability to translate complex theories into accessible insights, thereby training a new generation of thought leaders and specialists in both library science and technology. This multifaceted role, spanning teaching, research, and practice, has cemented his status as a **pioneer** whose influence extends well beyond traditional academic boundaries.

Dr. Elsherif's expertise and passion are truly global in scope. He has served as a **consultant to numerous educational institutions worldwide**, offering guidance on best practices, AI integration strategies, and effective management models. His international collaborations speak to the versatility of his knowledge, which is informed by a deep understanding of how AI can enhance resource discovery, user engagement, and scholarly communication across cultural and institutional contexts.

Central to Dr. Elsherif's mission is the belief that **innovative technologies**, including AI, must be harnessed responsibly and ethically. This commitment is evident in his approach to library management and educational technology, where he advocates for solutions that are inclusive, data-secure, and aligned with the core values of academic freedom and public service. By focusing on ethical implementation, he ensures that advancements in AI serve learners, educators, and researchers effectively and fairly.

Today, Dr. Elsherif continues to break new ground in **library innovation**, **academic research**, and **technology leadership**. Combining a passion for education with an unparalleled depth of knowledge, he remains a guiding force - **inspiring, educating, and leading** in library systems, educational institutions, and beyond. Through his work, he illuminates the path toward a future where AI seamlessly complements human expertise, thereby enriching the academic and public spheres for generations to come.

Preface

In the ever-evolving world of technology, the intersection of artificial intelligence and web development has opened up incredible possibilities. Just a few years ago, building an AI-powered website required a deep understanding of machine learning algorithms, complex infrastructure, and a team of developers. Today, thanks to platforms like Replit, it's possible for a single creator-with the right guidance-to bring intelligent, dynamic web applications to life from a single browser window.

This book was born out of a simple question: *How can we empower more people to build intelligent websites without needing to be AI experts or full-stack engineers?* Whether you're a developer curious about artificial intelligence, a student experimenting with projects, a startup founder building a prototype, or a teacher looking to bring AI into the classroom, this book is for you.

Mastering AI Web Development with Replit is designed to take you step-by-step through the process of building intelligent websites from scratch. We begin with the basics-understanding how Replit works and brushing up on foundational web development. From there, we introduce core AI concepts and tools, then move into practical integration with real APIs and real code. Each chapter builds on the last, guiding you from simple projects to more advanced, full-featured applications.

This book emphasizes hands-on practice. It's packed with real-world examples, guided exercises, and fully explained projects you can build and expand upon. You'll learn how to:

- Use Replit to write, test, and deploy websites
- Connect your frontend to AI models and APIs
- Accept payments and manage user data securely

- Deploy your projects on your own domain
- Optimize and scale your applications
- And much more

You don't need to be a professional developer to get started. If you can write basic HTML and follow instructions, you can follow along. If you're more advanced, you'll still find useful patterns, tools, and integrations to take your work to the next level.

As the author, my goal is not just to teach you how to build what's already been built-but to give you the skills and confidence to experiment, explore, and create something new. The future of the web is intelligent, and now is the perfect time to learn how to shape it.

Let's begin.

Hesham Mohamed Elsherif

Table of Contents

Chapter 1: Getting Started with Replit **15**

Creating an Account 15

Navigating the Interface 17

Understanding Replit Features 20

Setting Up Your First Repl 24

Customizing Your Environment 26

Chapter 2: Fundamental Web Development Concepts **30**

HTML Essentials 30

CSS Basics 33

JavaScript Introduction 37

Responsive Web Design Principles 40

Web Hosting and Deployment Basics 45

Chapter 3: Introduction to AI Technologies **50**

Types of AI Relevant to Web Development 53

Overview of Common AI Models 58

Ethical Considerations and Best Practices 65

Chapter 4: Integrating AI APIs **69**

Understanding APIs and Endpoints 69

Popular AI API Providers 75

Setting Up Environment Variables in Replit 81

Making API Requests from Your Website 85

Handling API Responses and Errors 91

Chapter 5: Building Your First AI-Powered Website **98**

Project Overview - AI Chatbot 98

Designing the User Interface 102

Connecting the Frontend to the Backend 106
Deploying and Testing Your AI Website 112
Chapter 6: Advanced AI Features 116
Implementing NLP 116
Adding Image Recognition 121
Using Generative AI for Content Creation 126
Building Recommendation Systems 131
Chapter 7: Enhancing User Interaction 138
Creating Dynamic and Interactive Elements 138
Managing User Input and AI Responses 145
Adding Real-Time Features 150
Improving UX and Accessibility 157
Chapter 8: Database Integration 164
Choosing and Setting Up Databases in Replit 164
CRUD Operations (Create, Read, Update, Delete) 169
Storing and Retrieving AI-Generated Data 174
Securing Data and Ensuring Privacy 181
Chapter 9: Integrating Payment Methods 186
Overview of Payment Gateway Options 186
Setting Up Payment APIs 191
Implementing Secure Transactions 198
Managing Subscriptions and Recurring Payments 203
Testing and Debugging Payment Systems 209
Chapter 10: Connecting to External Domains 216
Registering a Domain Name 216
Configuring DNS Settings 220
Linking Your Domain to Replit Projects 224

SSL Certificates and Secure Connections 228
Troubleshooting Domain Connection Issues 232
Chapter 11: Step-by-Step Practice Projects 237
AI-driven Weather Forecast Website 237
Real-Time Sentiment Analysis App 241
Intelligent Q&A Forum 246
Automated Content Moderation System 252
Performance-Optimization Techniques 262
Handling Traffic and Scaling Strategies 267
Monitoring and Analytics 273
Debugging and Maintenance Tips 280
Chapter 13: Troubleshooting Common Issues 287
Debugging AI Integrations 287
Common Replit Errors and Solutions 292
Troubleshooting Deployment Issues 297
Community Resources and Getting Help 302
Chapter 15: Next Steps and Continuous Learning 307
Staying Updated on AI Trends 307
Further Learning Resources 311
Advanced AI Techniques and Resources 315
Building a Career in AI Web Development 319
Appendices 326
Appendix A: Quick Reference Guide 326
Appendix B: Resources and Links 331
Appendix C: Glossary of Terms 338
Appendix D: Replit and AI Cheat Sheets 345

Introduction

Who Should Read This Book?

Building an AI-powered website once required a carefully orchestrated stack of servers, data pipelines, and machine-learning specialists. Today, a laptop, a browser, and an inquisitive mindset are enough to launch an intelligent web application-and Replit puts that power within easy reach. This book is written for anyone who wants to take advantage of that shift:

1. **Curious Self-Starters**
   You've dabbled in HTML, copied a few JavaScript snippets, or completed an online bootcamp and are ready to add "AI" to your skill set. The step-by-step projects will show you exactly where to start, what to build, and how to iterate.
2. **Working Web Developers & Designers**
   If you already craft front-end experiences or full-stack applications, you'll find practical patterns for integrating AI APIs, handling user data securely, and deploying to production-all without standing up new infrastructure.
3. **Students & Educators**
   Whether you're looking for a semester-long curriculum or a capstone idea, the guided chapters provide exercises that move from fundamentals to advanced techniques, complete with assessment checklists and extension challenges.
4. **Startup Founders & Product Managers**
   Need to validate an AI feature before investing developer months? You'll learn how to prototype chatbots, recommendation engines, and content generators quickly, then connect them to payments and custom domains.
5. **Career Switchers & Lifelong Learners**
   If you're transitioning into tech or simply hungry for new skills,

Replit's in-browser environment removes the friction of local setup. Each chapter ends with portfolio-ready deliverables you can demo to employers or clients.

6. **Hobbyists & Tinkerers**
   From automating a personal blog to powering a smart-home dashboard, the hands-on examples keep the process approachable-and fun.

If you can open a browser and have the curiosity to explore, this book will guide you from first prototype to production-ready AI website, one project at a time.

What You'll Learn

By the time you finish this book, you'll be able to plan, build, and deploy intelligent web applications entirely within Replit. We'll cover everything from front-end development basics to back-end logic and database integration, with AI features woven in throughout. Here's a breakdown of what you'll gain:

1. **Build Websites with Confidence**
   Learn to create and style modern websites using HTML, CSS, and JavaScript, all from inside Replit's browser-based environment.
2. **Understand AI Concepts That Matter**
   You don't need to be a data scientist to build AI-powered applications. This book walks you through practical concepts like NLP, computer vision, generative models, and recommendation engines-then shows you how to use them.
3. **Work with Real AI APIs**
   You'll use widely available services like OpenAI, Hugging Face, and others to bring intelligence to your websites. Learn how to make API calls, manage responses, and troubleshoot issues.
4. **Launch Functional AI Projects**
   Follow detailed, step-by-step guides to build apps like a chatbot,

image captioning tool, and a personalized content site-each designed to solidify your learning.

5. **Handle Payments and User Data**
   Set up secure payment processing using services like Stripe and PayPal, connect to databases for dynamic content, and ensure your site is secure and scalable.
6. **Deploy to Custom Domains**
   Take your projects live with custom domains and SSL certificates. You'll learn how to connect Replit projects to the wider internet and present a polished, professional product.
7. **Develop Practical Skills You Can Use Right Away**
   From debugging tips to UI improvements, each chapter provides real-world skills you can apply in freelance work, personal projects, or job interviews.

Whether you want to create the next AI-powered startup or just add smart features to your hobby project, this book gives you the tools and the roadmap to get there.

Why Choose Replit?

Replit is more than just an online code editor-it's a full-stack development environment in the browser. It was chosen as the foundation for this book because it eliminates many of the traditional barriers to web and AI development, making powerful tools accessible to anyone with an internet connection.

1. **No Setup Required**
   With Replit, you can start coding in seconds-no need to install packages, configure servers, or worry about your operating system. Whether you're using a Chromebook, tablet, or borrowed computer, you can access your projects and get to work immediately.
2. **Everything in One Place**
   Replit combines the features of an IDE, terminal, version control, deployment pipeline, and hosting platform into a single

interface. You can write code, test it, debug, and deploy-all without leaving the browser.

3. **Collaboration Made Simple**
   Just like Google Docs for code, Replit allows real-time collaboration. Invite others to view or edit your Repl, pair program, or share your work easily.
4. **Built-in Hosting and Deployment**
   With a click of a button, you can take your application live. This is especially useful for rapidly testing AI-powered features or demonstrating working prototypes to others.
5. **Access to AI Tools**
   Replit now offers its own set of AI features and supports integration with many third-party AI APIs. It's designed with the modern developer in mind, providing support for packages and tools commonly used in machine learning and natural language processing.
6. **Ideal for Learning and Experimentation**
   Because it removes so much of the friction associated with environment setup and devops, Replit is perfect for both beginners and advanced users who want to focus on experimenting, building, and learning.

In short, Replit puts powerful development tools at your fingertips-instantly. That's why it's the platform of choice for this book. Whether you're building your first project or deploying a polished AI web app, Replit gives you everything you need to get from idea to execution without leaving your browser.

Prerequisites and Tools

You don't need a degree in computer science or a background in artificial intelligence to get started with this book. However, a few basic skills and tools will help you get the most out of your learning experience:

1. **Basic Web Development Knowledge**
   You should be comfortable with basic HTML, CSS, and JavaScript. If you've created a simple web page before or followed an introductory course, you'll be in good shape. Don't worry-we'll revisit these fundamentals in early chapters.
2. **A Replit Account (Free or Pro)**
   All of the projects and exercises in this book are designed to run on Replit. You'll need to create a free Replit account at replit.com. If you want access to additional features like private Repls or more storage, consider using a Pro account, though it's not required.
3. **Internet Access**
   Since Replit runs in the cloud, a stable internet connection is essential. You won't need to install anything locally-just your browser and a network connection.
4. **A Modern Web Browser**
   Replit works best in Chrome, Firefox, or Edge. Safari is also supported but may have occasional layout issues. Make sure your browser is up to date for the best experience.
5. **API Access and Keys**
   To build AI features, you'll need to sign up for services like OpenAI, Hugging Face, or similar. These services provide API keys, which allow your projects to make AI requests. We'll walk through setting these up in the relevant chapters.
6. **Optional Tools**
   If you want to enhance your workflow, consider using a free GitHub account for version control, a tool like Postman to explore APIs, or a notes app to keep track of ideas and key snippets. None of these are mandatory, but they're helpful.

Everything else you need will be introduced along the way. This book is structured to be beginner-friendly without being oversimplified. If you bring a willingness to learn and a bit of time, you'll be surprised how much you can build.

Chapter 1: Getting Started with Replit

Creating an Account

Before you can build and deploy your own AI-powered websites on Replit, you'll need to create an account. Replit is a cloud-based platform, so all your projects (called "Repls") are stored online and accessible from any device with a browser.

Step 1: Go to Replit.com

Open your preferred web browser and navigate to:
https://replit.com

You'll land on the Replit homepage, which includes a "Sign up" or "Get started" button in the top right corner.

Step 2: Choose a Sign-Up Method

Click **Sign up**. You'll be offered several options:

- **Sign up with Google**
- **Sign up with GitHub**
- **Sign up with Apple**
- **Sign up with email**

Choose the method that's most convenient for you. If you're using this book in a classroom or work environment, Google or GitHub login can speed up account setup.

✅ **Tip:** If you plan to use GitHub for version control later, signing in with GitHub now can streamline integration.

Step 3: Create Your Username and Confirm Email

If you choose email signup, you'll be asked to:

- Enter your name
- Choose a unique username (e.g., ai-dev-jamie)
- Set a password
- Confirm your email address by clicking a verification link sent to your inbox

Replit uses your username as part of your project URLs (e.g., replit.com/@yourusername/projectname), so pick something you're comfortable sharing.

Step 4: Choose an Account Type

After signing in, Replit may ask whether you are a:

- **Student**
- **Teacher**
- **Hobbyist**
- **Professional developer**

This helps Replit tailor your experience, but it won't limit functionality. Choose the one that best describes your goals.

Step 5: Explore Your Dashboard

Once logged in, you'll land in the **Replit Dashboard**, which shows your past projects (if any), team workspaces, and a "Create" button to start a new Repl.

Here's what you'll see:

- **Top Navigation Bar** – with options like "My Repls," "Teams," and "Community"
- **Sidebar** – includes shortcuts to create Repls, view recent activity, and access account settings

- **Main Workspace** – where your project code and files will live once you start building

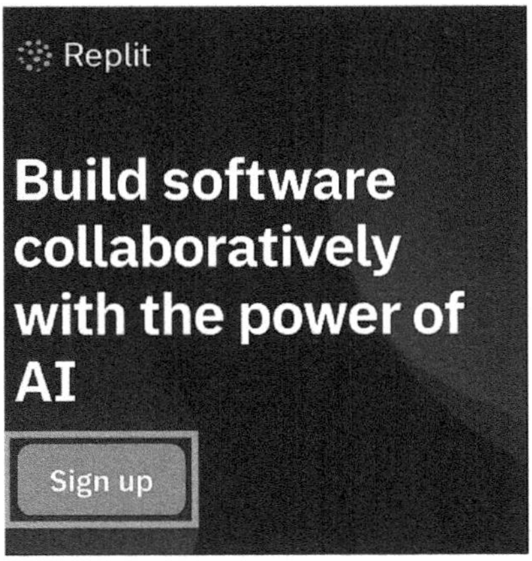

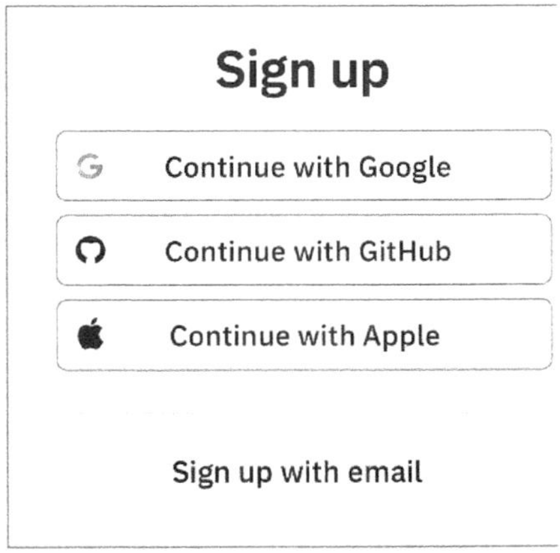

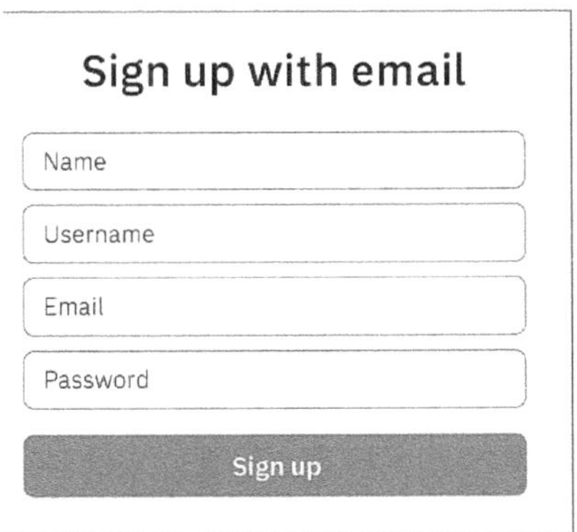

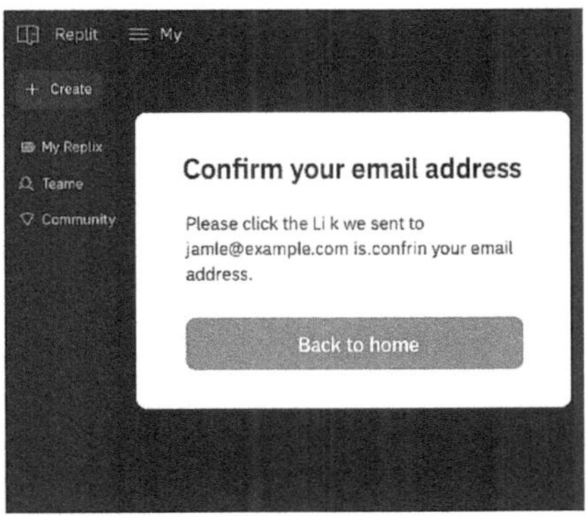

Navigating the Interface

Once you've created your Replit account and signed in, you'll land on the **Dashboard**. This is your starting point for every project and serves as the control panel for everything you build. Replit's interface is designed to be beginner-friendly while still powerful enough for advanced users.

Let's break it down into its key sections:

1. Top Navigation Bar

Located at the very top of the screen, this bar provides access to global features:

- **"+ Create" Button** – Start a new Repl (project) from scratch or from a template.
- **Search Bar** – Quickly find your existing Repls, templates, or public code shared by others.
- **Notifications Bell** – Alerts you to changes in shared projects or comments.
- **Profile Menu** – Access account settings, billing, and log out.

2. Left Sidebar

This is your primary workspace navigator:

- **My Repls** – View and open all your saved projects.
- **Teams** – Collaborate with classmates or coworkers in a shared space (great for classrooms).
- **Community** – Explore what others have built, fork interesting projects, or share your own.
- **Templates** – Browse common project setups, including HTML/CSS/JS, Python, Node.js, and more.
- **AI Tools (if enabled)** – Depending on your plan, you may see Replit AI tools like Ghostwriter.

3. Main Workspace

When you open a Repl, this is where development happens. It's split into three key panes:

- **Code Editor (Center Panel)**
  Where you write and edit files like index.html, main.py, or style.css. Tabs allow you to switch between files.
- **File Tree (Left Panel inside the Repl)**
  Shows your project's folder structure. You can create new files or folders, upload assets, or rename things here.
- **Preview & Output Panel (Right Panel)**
  Shows the results of your code. For web projects, this will display a live website preview. For Python or Node.js apps, it shows terminal output or console logs.

4. Bottom Tabs

These tools are context-sensitive:

- **Console** – Run commands, see logs, or interact with your app via the terminal.
- **Shell** – Access the full backend of your containerized Repl environment (great for advanced devs).
- **Debugger** – Step through code line-by-line to identify issues (available for supported languages).

5. Settings Gear (Top Right in a Repl)

Click this gear icon to change the theme (dark/light), font size, keybindings, and more. You can also configure environment variables or set up secrets here for secure API key storage.

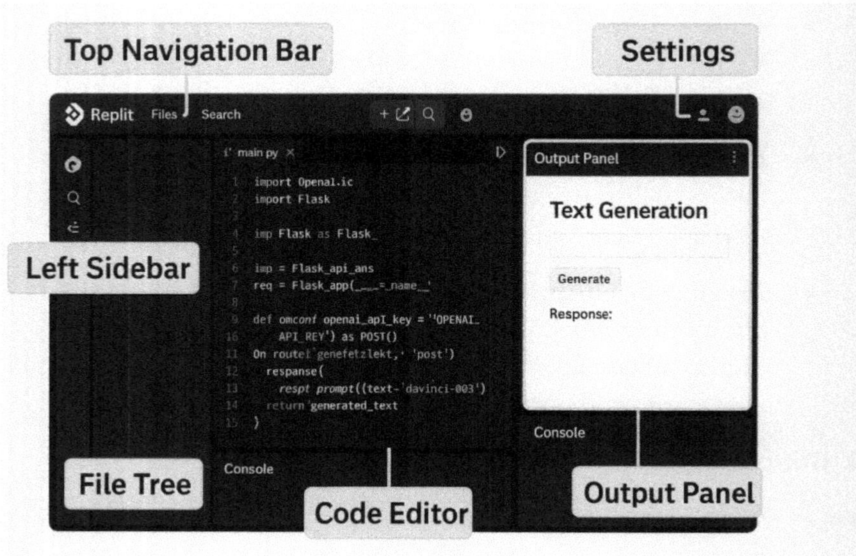

Understanding Replit Features

Replit isn't just an online code editor-it's a complete cloud-based development environment. Understanding its core features early on will help you make the most of the platform as you begin building intelligent web applications.

Below are the essential features that make Replit powerful for both beginners and experienced developers:

1. Multilanguage Support

Replit supports over 50 programming languages, including:

- **HTML/CSS/JavaScript** – for front-end web development
- **Python** – for AI scripts and APIs
- **Node.js** – for server-side applications

- **SQL, Bash, Java, C++, and more**
  You can switch languages easily by selecting a different template when creating a new Repl.

2. Zero-Setup Development

Replit eliminates the hassle of setting up local development environments. There's no need to install Python, Node, VS Code, or a local server:

- Code runs in the cloud.
- Your browser becomes your IDE.
- Projects are ready to run instantly.

This is especially helpful for AI projects, which often require tricky dependencies.

3. Instant Hosting and Deployment

Every Repl can be instantly deployed and shared via a live URL:

- Click "Run" to host your app.
- Use the "Share" button to get a public link.
- Great for testing and showing progress to others.

You can also deploy to custom domains and even set up HTTPS with a few clicks.

4. Built-In Terminal and Console

Each Repl includes:

- A **console** for output (great for debugging print statements or AI responses).
- A **shell/terminal** for running commands, managing files, or installing packages manually using pip, npm, etc.

5. Package Manager

Replit detects your code and helps manage dependencies automatically. You can:

- Install Python packages with pip or via the sidebar UI.
- Use Node.js package.json to install modules like express, axios, or dotenv.

This makes integrating AI libraries or third-party APIs a lot easier.

6. Version Control and GitHub Integration

Replit tracks your changes automatically, but you can also:

- Link your Repls to a GitHub repository.
- Push/pull commits directly from the browser.

It's a great way to learn Git workflows without using the command line.

7. AI and Ghostwriter (Optional)

With a Pro account, you get access to **Ghostwriter**, Replit's built-in AI assistant. It can:

- Suggest code completions
- Explain errors
- Generate boilerplate code

Even without Ghostwriter, you can use external AI APIs (like OpenAI) with the tools we cover in this book.

8. Secrets Management

To safely store sensitive data like API keys:

- Use Replit's **Secrets tab** to create secure environment variables.
- Your keys won't be exposed in public code or when sharing your Repl.

We'll make extensive use of this when connecting to AI services.

9. Real-Time Collaboration

Invite others to co-edit a Repl-like Google Docs for code. Use this for:

- Pair programming
- Classroom collaboration
- Team debugging

All collaborators see changes in real time and can chat inside the project window.

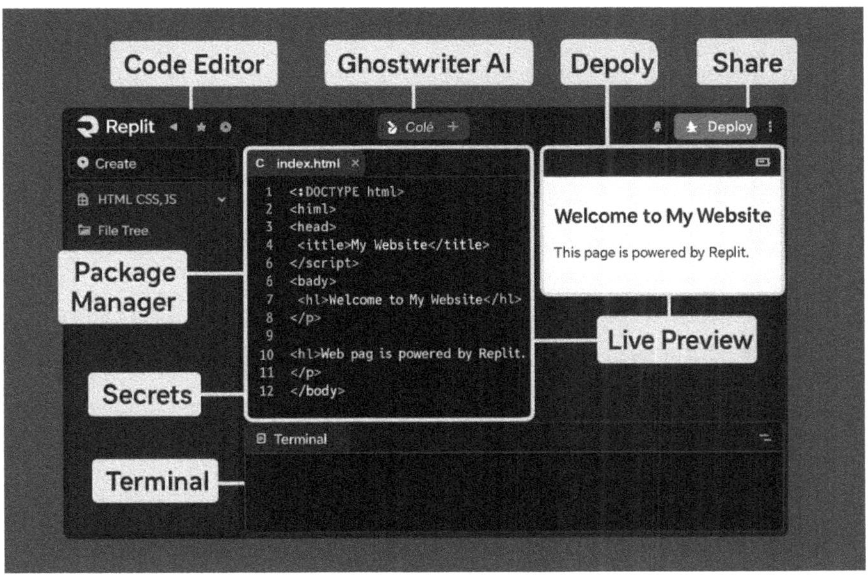

Setting Up Your First Repl

A **Repl** (short for "read-eval-print loop") is the core unit of a project on Replit. It's where your files, code editor, runtime, and preview window all come together. Setting up your first Repl is quick and straightforward-and it gives you everything you need to start coding and testing immediately.

Follow these steps to create your first Repl:

Step 1: Click "+ Create" from the Dashboard

After logging in to your Replit account, look for the **+ Create** button on the top left of the dashboard or navigation bar. Clicking this opens the Repl creation modal.

Step 2: Choose a Template

You'll be prompted to select a language or template to base your project on. Some popular choices include:

- **HTML, CSS, JS** – for front-end websites
- **Python** – for scripting, AI bots, or backend logic
- **Node.js** – for full-stack JavaScript applications
- **Replit AI Templates** – if available in your plan, these include pre-built AI integration examples

For this book's first example, choose **HTML, CSS, JS**.

Step 3: Name Your Repl

You'll need to give your project a name. Replit will suggest a random one like sparkling-octopus, but you can change it to something descriptive like my-first-ai-site.

Your Repl's public URL will use this name:
https://replit.com/@yourusername/my-first-ai-site

✅ **Tip:** Repls can be renamed later, but it's good to start with something clear.

Step 4: Set Project Visibility

You can choose to make the Repl:

- **Public** (visible and searchable to everyone)
- **Private** (only accessible to you or invited collaborators-requires a Pro account)

For now, Public is fine unless you're handling sensitive code or keys.

Step 5: Click "Create Repl"

Once you've selected a template, named your Repl, and chosen visibility, click the **Create Repl** button. Replit will now:

- Initialize your coding environment
- Load boilerplate files (e.g., index.html, style.css, script.js)
- Open the editor, console, and preview window

You're now ready to start building your project.

What's Next?

From here, you can:

- Modify the HTML to add a headline or button
- Use the Preview panel to see changes live
- Click **Run** to host the page temporarily
- Share the live link with others

Every Repl comes with automatic version saving, so you can close your browser and return later without losing work.

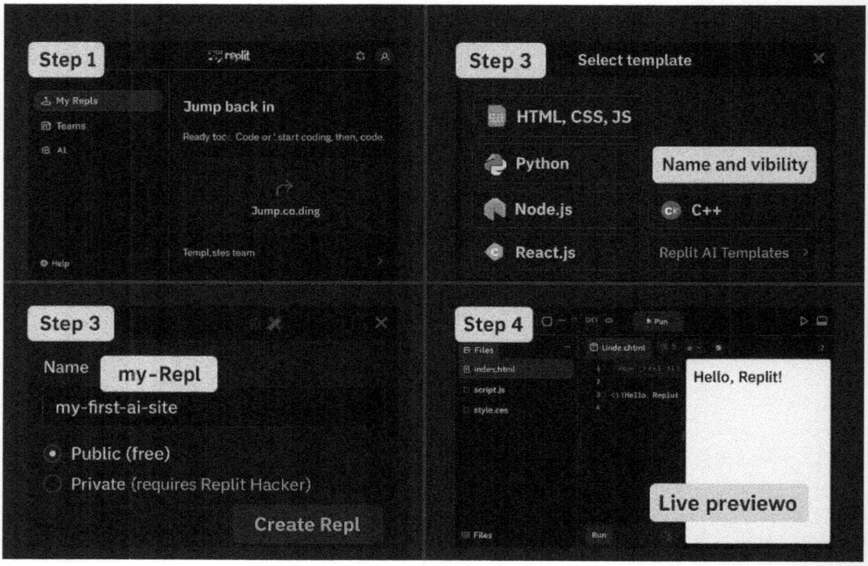

Customizing Your Environment

Replit provides a flexible and user-friendly development environment that works right from your browser-but it's also highly customizable. Personalizing your environment helps improve your focus, productivity, and comfort during long coding sessions.

This section walks you through the most important settings you can tailor to your workflow.

1. Changing the Theme (Dark or Light Mode)

Replit supports both dark and light themes. Here's how to switch:

- Click the **gear icon** (⚙) in the top-right corner of any open Repl.
- In the **"Editor settings"** panel, toggle between **Dark** and **Light** themes.

💡 Tip: Dark mode is easier on the eyes for long coding sessions or late-night work.

2. Adjusting Font Size and Spacing

You can customize the text display to match your visual preference:

- Under **Editor Settings**, you'll see options for:
    - **Font Size** – Small, medium, large
    - **Line Height** – Adjust vertical spacing
    - **Word Wrap** – Automatically wrap long lines
    - **Indentation Width** – Change tab size (e.g., 2 or 4 spaces)

Choose the combination that feels clean and readable for you.

3. Choosing Keybindings

If you're used to another editor like VS Code or Vim, Replit lets you bring over familiar shortcuts:

- Navigate to **Editor Settings → Keybindings**
- Choose from:
    - **Default**
    - **Vim** (for modal editing)
    - **Emacs**
    - **Sublime Text**

This allows you to retain your existing muscle memory and speed.

4. Installing Extensions and Packages

For supported languages like Python or Node.js, you can add tools and libraries directly:

- In the **Package Manager** (left sidebar):

    - Search and install packages like flask, pandas, or express
    - Replit automatically adds these to your project's environment
- Use the **Secrets tab** to manage API keys and environment variables securely

5. Using the Shell and Console

Replit includes:

- A **Console**, for logging output and seeing runtime errors
- A **Shell**, for typing terminal commands like pip install, git init, or npm run

You can customize which of these opens by default under your **Workspace settings**.

6. Setting Up a .replit File (Advanced)

For advanced users, Replit includes a special configuration file:

- The .replit file allows you to:
    - Define custom run commands
    - Set a different default file to launch (e.g., app.py instead of main.py)
    - Specify a language or interpreter manually

This is especially useful when building more complex AI or multi-language projects.

7. Custom Layout and Tabs

You can:

- Split the code editor into multiple tabs

- Resize the preview and terminal panels
- Pin frequently used files

This flexibility lets you design a layout that fits your coding style-whether you prefer full-screen editing, live preview, or side-by-side coding and logs.

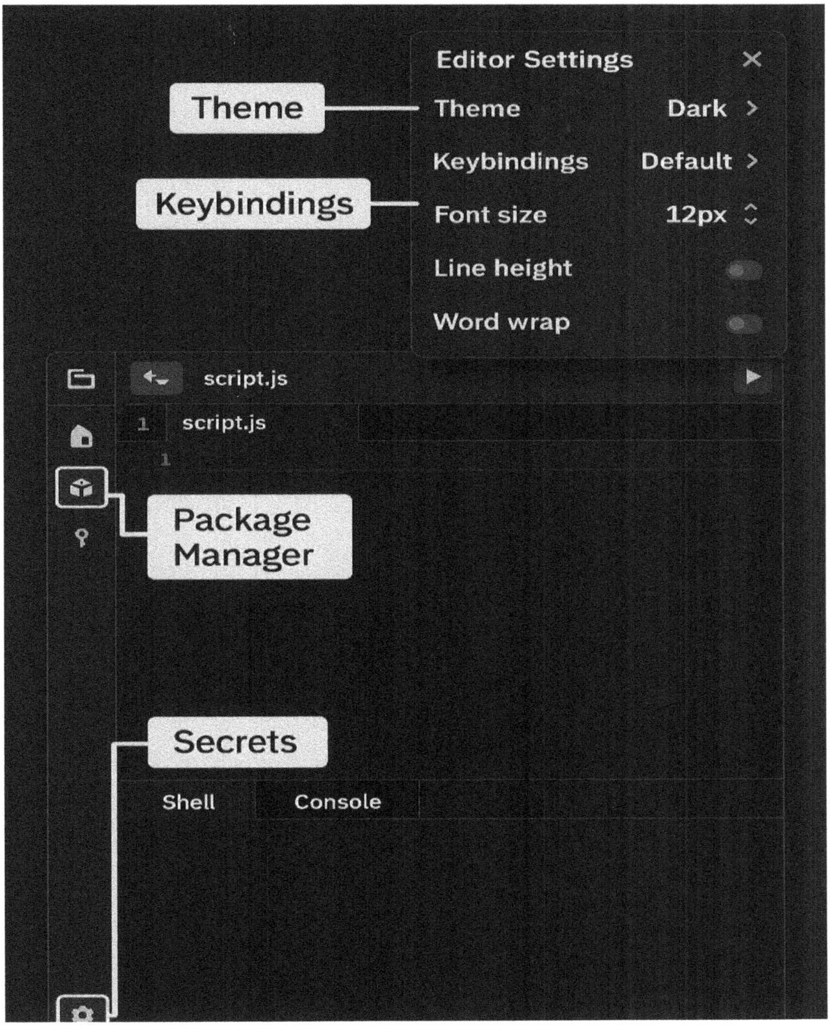

Chapter 2: Fundamental Web Development Concepts

HTML Essentials

HTML (HyperText Markup Language) is the foundation of every website. It structures the content users see and interact with-headings, paragraphs, images, buttons, links, and more. Understanding how HTML works is the first step to building functional AI-powered sites.

Replit makes it easy to write, preview, and experiment with HTML, so let's explore the essentials.

What HTML Does

HTML provides a **structure** for your webpage by using **elements**, each enclosed in **tags**. A typical HTML document includes:

```
<!DOCTYPE html>
<html>
  <head>
    <title>My First AI Website</title>
  </head>
  <body>
    <h1>Hello, world!</h1>
    <p>This site uses AI to generate content.</p>
  </body>
</html>
```

Core HTML Elements

Here are the most commonly used elements you'll work with:

Tag	Purpose
<html>	Wraps the entire page
<head>	Contains meta info, scripts, title
<body>	Visible page content lives here
<h1> to <h6>	Headings, with <h1> being the largest
<p>	Paragraph text
<a href="URL">	Creates links
<img src="URL" alt="desc">	Displays an image
<div> and <span>	Generic containers for layout and styling
<button>	Adds a clickable button

Attributes

Most HTML tags accept **attributes**-extra information inside the opening tag. For example:

<a href="https://openai.com" target="_blank">Visit OpenAI</a>

- href defines the link destination
- target="_blank" opens it in a new tab

Attributes are key when integrating forms, AI scripts, or interactive elements.

Nesting and Structure

HTML is hierarchical. Tags must be opened and closed properly, and elements can contain other elements:

```
<div>
  <h2>AI Summary</h2>
  <p>This content is generated dynamically using OpenAI's API.</p>
</div>
```

This nesting allows you to create modular content blocks, which is critical for AI-driven interfaces.

Best Practices

- Always include a <!DOCTYPE html> declaration at the top.
- Use semantic tags (<header>, <footer>, <section>, <article>) when possible for accessibility and SEO.
- Indent nested elements for readability.
- Close all tags-even if the browser is forgiving.

Using HTML in Replit

When you create a new **HTML, CSS, JS** Repl:

- You'll see `index.html`, `style.css`, and `script.js`.
- Modify `index.html` to add content.
- Click **Run** to preview your page instantly.

Try changing the `<h1>` text to your name and see the browser update live.

CSS Basics

CSS (Cascading Style Sheets) controls the **appearance and layout** of your web page. While HTML handles structure and content, CSS is what makes your site visually appealing-from fonts and colors to positioning and animations.

Learning basic CSS will help you turn your functional Replit projects into clean, modern interfaces that users will enjoy interacting with.

How CSS Works

CSS styles are rules applied to HTML elements. Each rule has:

- A **selector** that targets the element
- A **property** that defines what to change
- A **value** for that property

Example:

```
h1 {
  color: blue;
  font-size: 32px;
}
```

This tells the browser: "make all <h1> elements blue and 32 pixels tall."

Ways to Add CSS

1. **Inline CSS** – inside HTML tags

```
<p style="color: red;">Warning!</p>
```

2. **Internal CSS** – inside a <style> tag in the HTML <head>

```
<style>
 body {
  background-color: #f9f9f9;
 }
</style>
```

3. **External CSS** – in a separate file (most common in Replit) Example from style.css:

```
p {
 line-height: 1.5;
```

}

Then link it in your HTML:

<link rel="stylesheet" href="style.css">

In Replit's HTML template, this link is already included by default.

Common CSS Properties

Property	Example Value	Purpose
color	#333, blue	Text color
background	#fff, url(...)	Background color or image
font-size	16px, 2em	Controls text size
margin	20px, auto	Space outside the element
padding	10px	Space inside the element
border	1px solid #000	Draws a border around the element
display	block, flex	Controls layout behavior

CSS Selectors

- * – targets everything
- h1, p – targets all of that tag
- .classname – targets elements with that class
- #idname – targets a specific element with an ID
- div > p – targets <p> directly inside a <div>

Example:

```
.container {
  max-width: 800px;
  margin: 0 auto;
}
```

Using CSS in Replit

In a Replit HTML/CSS/JS Repl:

- Edit style.css for styles
- Use class="..." or id="..." in your HTML
- Hit **Run** and view updates live in the preview pane

Try customizing the background or text colors to match the feel of your AI project.

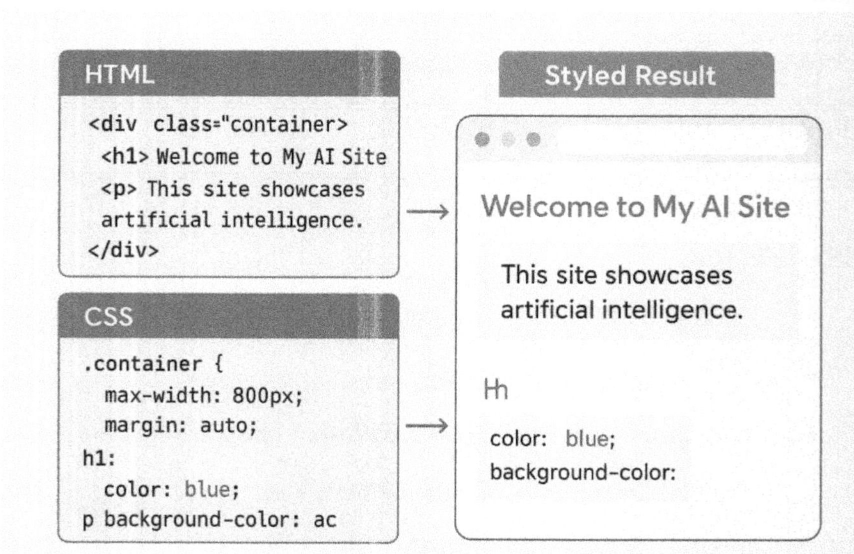

JavaScript Introduction

JavaScript is a core part of modern web development, especially when building intelligent or AI-powered websites. Alongside HTML (structure) and CSS (styling), JavaScript brings websites to life with interactivity, logic, and real-time behavior. If you're building on platforms like Replit, understanding how JavaScript fits into the bigger picture is essential before layering in AI capabilities.

What is JavaScript?

JavaScript is a scripting language that runs in the browser and powers dynamic content on web pages. Whenever a website responds to user input, updates content without reloading, or interacts with APIs-including AI APIs like OpenAI or Hugging Face-JavaScript is behind it.

Unlike HTML and CSS, JavaScript is a full-fledged programming language. It handles:

- Logic and decision-making (if, else, switch)
- Interactions (click, input, submit)
- Data manipulation (arrays, objects, loops)
- Asynchronous operations (like fetching data from an API)

Core Concepts in JavaScript for Web Development

1. DOM Manipulation

The DOM (Document Object Model) is the tree-like structure browsers use to interpret HTML. JavaScript lets you read, modify, or react to changes in the DOM.

```
document.getElementById("myButton").addEventListener("click",
function() {
  alert("Button clicked!");
```

```
});
```

2. Variables and Data Types

JavaScript is loosely typed and supports several variable types:

```
let name = "AI Assistant"; // string
let age = 5;               // number
let isActive = true;       // Boolean
```

3. Functions

Functions allow you to encapsulate reusable logic. They're central to AI workflows where repeated processing happens, like parsing API results.

```
function greetUser(name) {
   return `Hello, ${name}`;
}
```

4. Events and User Interaction

Events are key to building interactive interfaces:

```
document.querySelector("#ask").addEventListener("click", () => {
   console.log("Question sent!");
});
```

5. Asynchronous JavaScript (Async/Await)

When calling AI APIs or loading data from a server, JavaScript uses asynchronous code to avoid freezing the interface.

```
async function fetchAIResponse(prompt) {
   const response = await fetch("https://api.example.com/ai", {
```

```
    method: "POST",
    body: JSON.stringify({ prompt }),
  });
  const data = await response.json();
  return data.output;
}
```

How JavaScript Fits into AI Web Development on Replit

Replit offers a full-stack development environment where you can write HTML, CSS, and JavaScript all in one place. You can also easily add backend functionality using Node.js (which is JavaScript on the server). For AI projects, this means:

- Creating a frontend interface in HTML/CSS
- Using JavaScript to capture user input and send it to an AI API
- Handling the response and updating the DOM with the AI's output
- Optionally adding a backend with Node.js to manage API keys securely

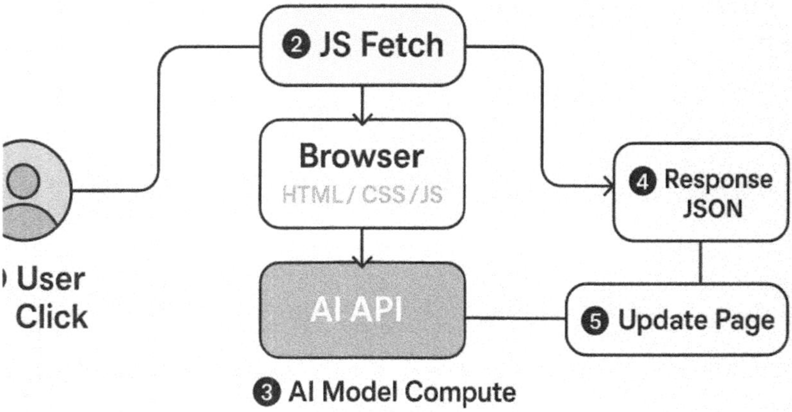

Responsive Web Design Principles

Building intelligent websites isn't just about adding AI APIs and logic. If your site doesn't look and feel right across all devices-phones, tablets, desktops-users will bounce before they ever interact with your AI. This is where **Responsive Web Design (RWD)** comes in.

What Is Responsive Web Design?

Responsive Web Design is an approach to building websites that automatically adapt to different screen sizes and orientations. Whether someone visits your site on a laptop or a smartphone, it should remain functional, readable, and visually appealing without requiring zooming or horizontal scrolling.

RWD is not just a trend-it's a standard. As AI becomes part of real-world interfaces (like smart assistants, AI chat widgets, or recommendation systems), responsiveness ensures that your intelligent UI is usable everywhere.

Key Principles of Responsive Web Design

1. Fluid Grids

Instead of using fixed pixel widths, responsive layouts use percentages. This allows content to resize proportionally.

```
.container {
   width: 100%;
   max-width: 1200px;
   margin: 0 auto;
}
```

2. Flexible Images

Images should scale with the layout rather than overflow or break it.

```
img {
   max-width: 100%;
   height: auto;
}
```

3. Media Queries

Media queries are a core feature of CSS that let you apply different styles depending on screen size or device type.

```
@media (max-width: 768px) {
   .sidebar {
      display: none;
   }
```

```
  .main-content {
    width: 100%;
  }
}
```

This CSS hides the sidebar and expands the main content area on devices narrower than 768px (e.g., phones and small tablets).

4. Mobile-First Design

Mobile-first means designing your layout for smaller screens first, then enhancing it for larger ones using media queries. This approach is more efficient and aligns better with how most users access the web today.

```
/* Base styles for mobile */
body {
  font-size: 16px;
  padding: 10px;
}


/* Enhanced styles for larger screens */
@media (min-width: 768px) {
  body {
    font-size: 18px;
    padding: 20px;
  }
}
```

5. Viewport Meta Tag

This tag ensures your design behaves properly on mobile browsers.

```
<meta name="viewport" content="width=device-width, initial-scale=1.0">
```

Without this, your page might render zoomed out or not scale as intended.

Why It Matters in AI Web Development

If your AI features-like a chatbot, visual assistant, or interactive recommender-aren't responsive, they become useless on mobile. Responsive design ensures:

- Your chat UI doesn't spill off screen
- AI responses remain readable
- Interactions feel native on any device
- Voice/gesture integrations (if any) align properly with layout

Responsive Layout for an AI Chat App (Example)

Here's a simple structure:

```
<div class="chat-container">
  <div class="chat-messages"></div>
  <input type="text" placeholder="Ask something..." />
</div>

.chat-container {
  width: 100%;
  max-width: 600px;
  margin: auto;
```

```
  padding: 1rem;
}

@media (max-width: 480px) {
  .chat-container {
    padding: 0.5rem;
  }
}
```

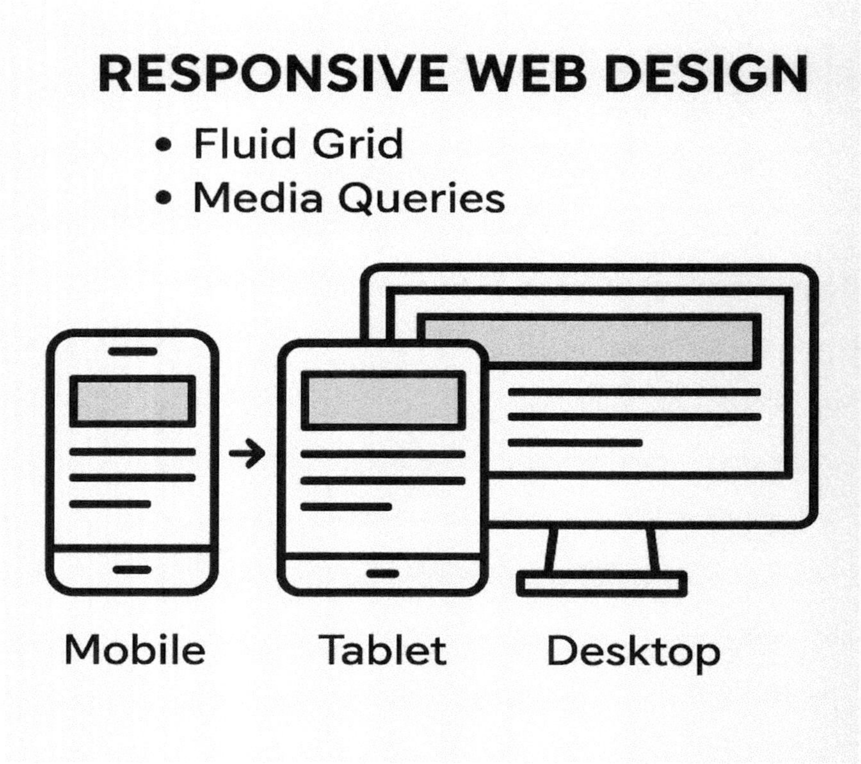

Web Hosting and Deployment Basics

Once you've built your intelligent website-complete with HTML, CSS, JavaScript, and AI-powered features-the next step is to make it accessible to the world. That's where **web hosting and deployment** come in.

What Is Web Hosting?

Web hosting refers to the service of storing your website's files on a server and making them accessible via the internet. When someone visits your site (e.g., yourname.replit.app), their browser sends a request to that server, which responds with your web content.

In simple terms, hosting is like renting a plot of land where your website lives.

What Is Deployment?

Deployment is the act of transferring your website from a development environment (like Replit's workspace) to a live server where users can access it.

For AI-powered projects, deployment often includes:

- Hosting both front-end (UI) and back-end (server-side logic)
- Managing API keys securely
- Ensuring scalability for real-time AI responses

Hosting and Deployment with Replit

Replit simplifies both steps. It lets you:

- Write and test code in one place (browser-based IDE)
- Instantly deploy your project with a click
- Share your site via a public URL (like yourproject.replit.app)

How It Works:

1. You create a Replit project (called a "Repl").
2. You write your code: HTML, CSS, JavaScript, and optionally, Node.js.
3. Replit runs a lightweight server behind the scenes.
4. When you click "Run" or "Deploy," Replit:
    - Starts the server
    - Hosts your files
    - Gives you a live URL for public access

Common Deployment Scenarios

1. Static Websites

These are sites with only front-end code (HTML/CSS/JS), often using AI APIs from the browser.

- Deployment is as easy as writing code in index.html, clicking **Run**, and sharing your Replit link.

2. Full-Stack Apps

If your project includes a backend (e.g., a Node.js server for storing data or routing API requests), Replit can handle this too.

- You set up server.js to handle requests.
- Replit keeps it running and connected to your front-end.

3. AI-Powered Projects

- You can store API keys in Replit Secrets to keep them hidden from users.

- Backend code can route requests to OpenAI, Hugging Face, or other AI services.

Example structure:

index.html → Frontend layout

style.css → Visual design

script.js → Frontend logic (calls API)

server.js → Backend proxy for AI API

.replit → Defines run command

.env (Secrets) → API keys (hidden from frontend)

Key Hosting Concepts

Concept	**Description**
Server	A computer that hosts your website and responds to browser requests.
Domain Name	The human-readable address of your site (e.g., yourproject.replit.app).
DNS	Connects your domain name to your Replit server.
Deployment	The process of pushing code to a live environment.
Environment Variables	Hidden values (like API keys) stored securely.

Publishing Your Replit Site (Step-by-Step)

1. **Create a Repl** (choose HTML, Node.js, or your preferred stack).
2. **Write your code** (UI, backend logic, AI integration).
3. **Use Secrets** to securely store any API keys or config values.
4. **Test it** locally in the Replit browser window.
5. **Click "Deploy"** from the Replit menu.
6. **Copy and share** your live URL.

When to Consider External Hosting

While Replit is great for development and lightweight apps, you might outgrow it if:

- You need advanced server control or database integration.
- You expect high traffic and want to scale aggressively.
- You need custom domains (outside of replit.app) with SSL.

In those cases, you can export your code and host it on platforms like:

- Vercel or Netlify (for front-end)
- Heroku or Render (for full-stack apps)
- AWS, DigitalOcean, or Azure (for enterprise-level control)

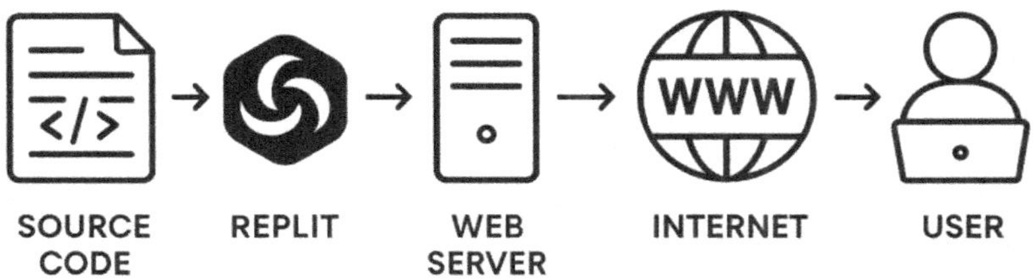

WEB HOSTING DEPLOYMENT

Chapter 3: Introduction to AI Technologies

What is Artificial Intelligence?

Before you build intelligent websites, it's important to understand what powers the "intelligence" behind them. At its core, **Artificial Intelligence (AI)** refers to the ability of a machine or software to perform tasks that typically require human intelligence.

That includes things like:

- Understanding natural language
- Recognizing images or speech
- Making decisions based on data
- Learning from experience (improving over time)

In web development, AI allows us to build features that can *understand*, *predict*, and *interact*-from chatbots and recommendation systems to auto-generating content or analyzing user behavior in real-time.

Defining AI: A Practical Perspective

Artificial Intelligence is not a single technology. It's an umbrella term that includes various subfields:

- **Machine Learning (ML)** – systems that learn from data
- **Natural Language Processing (NLP)** – understanding and generating human language
- **Computer Vision** – interpreting visual information (images, video)
- **Expert Systems** – rule-based decision-making engines

- **Generative AI** – models that create new text, code, images, etc.

So, when you ask a chatbot a question and it responds like a human, or when a web app recommends a product based on your browsing history-that's AI in action.

AI in the Context of Web Development

In traditional websites, developers write explicit rules: *"If the user clicks this button, do X."*

With AI:

- Systems infer what the user wants based on context, patterns, or predictions.
- Behavior is driven by data rather than hard-coded rules.
- The website can **adapt**, **respond**, and **improve** without manual updates.

Examples of AI in web apps:

- A chatbot built with OpenAI's GPT API that answers customer questions
- A personalized movie recommendation feed using collaborative filtering
- An image classifier that tags uploaded photos in a gallery
- A summarizer that condenses long articles using NLP

Symbolic AI vs. Machine Learning

There are two main approaches to AI:

Approach	Description
Symbolic AI	Logic-based. Uses human-defined rules (e.g., IF X, THEN Y). Often seen in early expert systems.
Machine Learning	Data-driven. Learns patterns from large datasets. Powers modern NLP, computer vision, and generative AI.

Why It Matters for You

As a developer, you don't need a PhD to use AI. Thanks to tools like Replit and AI APIs, you can integrate powerful models with just a few lines of JavaScript.

This means:

- You can build smarter features faster.
- You can experiment without deep math.
- You can customize AI behavior to fit your site's needs.

It's less about understanding *how* the entire brain works, and more about knowing *how to ask smart questions and use the tools well.*

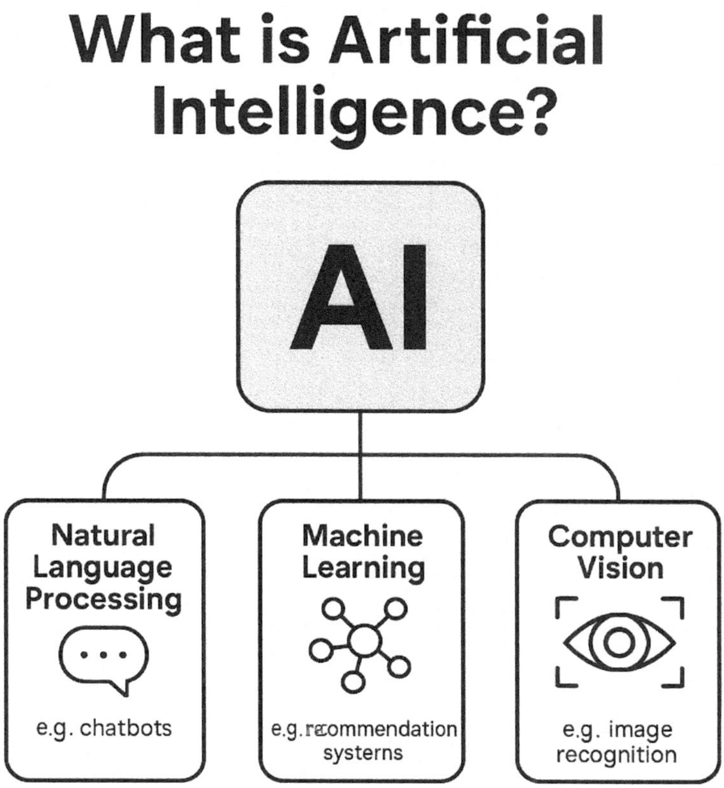

Types of AI Relevant to Web Development

Artificial Intelligence (AI) spans a broad field, but not every AI concept applies directly to web development. In the context of building intelligent websites, certain types of AI stand out as especially useful, practical, and often easy to integrate using modern APIs and frameworks.

This section breaks down the **key types of AI that web developers should know**, with real-world relevance and implementation examples using tools like JavaScript, Node.js, and Replit.

1. Natural Language Processing (NLP)

What it is:
NLP enables machines to read, understand, interpret, and generate human language. It bridges the gap between structured code and natural communication.

How it applies to the web:

- Chatbots and virtual assistants
- Text summarization
- Sentiment analysis on user reviews
- Auto-reply suggestions or autocomplete

Example use case on Replit:
Using OpenAI's GPT API to power a customer support chatbot that understands and responds naturally in conversation.

```
const response = await
fetch('https://api.openai.com/v1/chat/completions', { /* ... */ });
```

2. Machine Learning (ML)

What it is:
ML refers to algorithms that learn from data to make predictions or decisions without being explicitly programmed for every case.

How it applies to the web:

- Product recommendations
- Fraud detection systems
- Predictive input fields (e.g., form suggestions)
- Behavior-based personalization

Example use case on Replit:
A recommendation engine that uses past user actions to show smarter content suggestions, using a pre-trained model hosted as an API.

3. Computer Vision

What it is:
Computer Vision (CV) allows machines to interpret and analyze visual data like images and video.

How it applies to the web:

- Image upload filters and tag suggestions
- Face detection in profile images
- OCR (optical character recognition) in scanned documents
- AR try-on features for e-commerce

Example use case on Replit:
A web app that lets users upload an image and receive AI-generated tags or descriptions using a vision API like Google Vision or Hugging Face.

4. Speech Recognition and Generation

What it is:
Speech technologies convert spoken language into text (speech-to-text) or produce speech from text (text-to-speech).

How it applies to the web:

- Voice-enabled navigation or search
- AI voice assistants in-browser
- Real-time transcription
- Interactive audio guides or accessibility tools

Example use case on Replit:
Integrating Web Speech API or a third-party service like AssemblyAI to let users talk to your app and receive voice feedback.

5. Generative AI

What it is:
Generative AI creates new content-text, code, images, audio-based on patterns it has learned from data. It uses models like GPT (text), DALL·E (images), and Codex (code).

How it applies to the web:

- Blog post generation
- Image generation tools
- Code autocomplete for developer-focused sites
- AI-powered creative writing tools

Example use case on Replit:
A web-based prompt-to-image generator using the DALL·E API, where users type a description and get a visual result instantly.

Comparison Summary

AI Type	Common Web Uses	Tools & APIs
NLP	Chatbots, sentiment analysis, summarization	OpenAI, Cohere, Hugging Face
ML	Recommendations, predictions, classifications	TensorFlow.js, Python API backends
Computer Vision	Image tagging, face recognition, OCR	Google Vision, Clarifai, Hugging Face

AI Type	Common Web Uses	Tools & APIs
Speech Technologies	Voice input/output, transcription	Web Speech API, AssemblyAI
Generative AI	Text, image, or code creation	OpenAI, DALL·E, Replicate

Why These AI Types Matter

The most valuable websites today are not just interactive-they're intelligent. Choosing the right type of AI to integrate depends on your use case:

- Need your site to understand language? Use **NLP**.
- Need your app to "see"? Use **Computer Vision**.
- Want to personalize content dynamically? Use **ML**.
- Want to enable voice commands? Use **Speech AI**.
- Want to generate content? Use **Generative AI**.

And with tools like Replit and cloud-based APIs, you don't need to train these models yourself-you can plug them in and go.

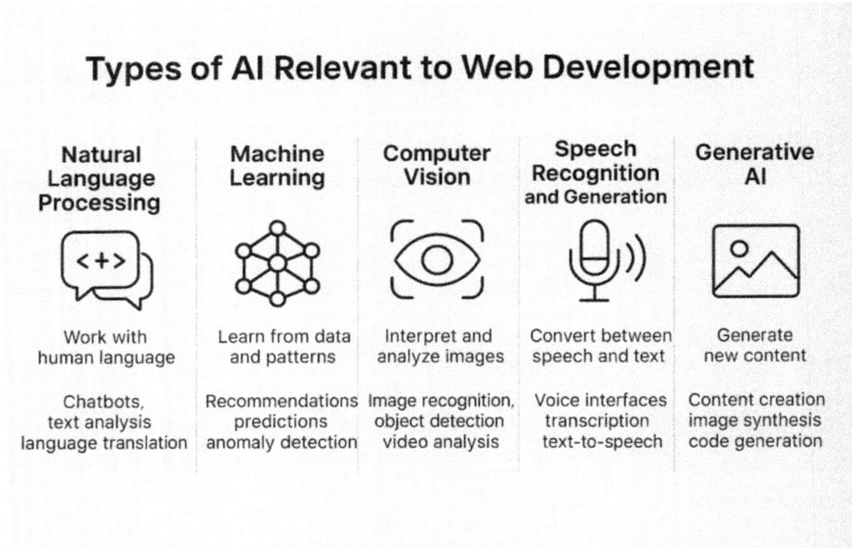

Overview of Common AI Models

To build AI-powered websites, you don't need to train your own models from scratch. Today, many powerful AI models are available via APIs, and they're easy to integrate with tools like Replit. But to use them effectively, it helps to understand what each model is good at and how it works in broad terms.

Below is an overview of the **most common AI model types** relevant to web development. These are the engines behind chatbots, content generators, recommendation tools, and more.

1. Large Language Models (LLMs)

Examples:

- OpenAI's GPT-4
- Google Gemini (formerly Bard)
- Meta's LLaMA

- Cohere Command R

What They Do:
LLMs are trained on massive text datasets to understand and generate human-like language. They're the backbone of intelligent chatbots, text generators, auto-responders, and more.

Common Use Cases in Web Development:

- Customer service bots
- Content generation (blog posts, summaries)
- Semantic search
- Language translation
- Form autofill based on natural language input

How to Use on Replit:
Connect to OpenAI's API via fetch() in JavaScript or via a Node.js backend using axios.

2. Text-to-Image Models

Examples:

- DALL·E (OpenAI)
- Stable Diffusion (Stability AI)
- Midjourney

What They Do:
These models generate images from descriptive text prompts. Great for visual creativity tools and user-generated content features.

Common Use Cases:

- AI art generators
- Product mockup tools

- Educational or storytelling platforms

How to Use on Replit:
Use prompt input from users, send it to a model API (e.g. DALL·E), and display the generated image directly in the browser.

3. Vision Models

Examples:

- Google Vision AI
- OpenCV (classic library)
- CLIP (OpenAI – connects text and image understanding)

What They Do:
These models analyze images to detect objects, extract text, or recognize faces and scenes.

Common Use Cases:

- Image tagging
- Face or object detection
- OCR (extracting text from images)
- Content moderation (e.g. NSFW detection)

How to Use:
Upload images via a form and send them to a vision API. Return labeled results or detected features to display on the page.

4. Speech Models

Examples:

- Whisper (OpenAI – speech-to-text)
- Google Speech-to-Text / Text-to-Speech

- AssemblyAI

What They Do:
These models convert spoken audio to text or vice versa. They enable voice interfaces in web applications.

Common Use Cases:

- Voice-enabled chatbots or navigation
- Real-time transcription
- Audio summaries or accessibility features

How to Use:
Use the Web Speech API for client-side recognition or connect to cloud APIs for better accuracy and multiple language support.

5. Recommendation Models

Examples:

- Collaborative Filtering (Netflix, Amazon)
- Matrix Factorization
- Transformer-based ranking models

What They Do:
These models suggest items based on user preferences or behavior patterns. While less "flashy" than LLMs, they are essential for personalization.

Common Use Cases:

- Product or content recommendations
- Personalized news feeds
- "Customers also bought" sections

How to Use:

Start with simple heuristics or integrate a recommendation engine via APIs or pretrained ML models (Python backend with Flask or FastAPI on Replit).

Summary Table

AI Model Type	Example APIs / Models	Primary Use Cases in Web Dev
Large Language Models	GPT-4, Gemini, Cohere	Chatbots, text generation
Text-to-Image	DALL·E, Stable Diffusion	Image generation from prompts
Vision Models	Google Vision, CLIP	Image tagging, OCR
Speech Models	Whisper, Google Speech	Voice input/output, transcripts
Recommendation Models	Custom ML, TensorFlow	Product/content suggestions

Choosing the Right Model

When adding AI to your website, ask:

- Do I need to understand or generate **text**? → Use an LLM.
- Do I want to generate **images**? → Use a text-to-image model.
- Is the user uploading or interacting with **photos**? → Use a vision model.

- Is the interaction based on **voice**? → Use a speech model.
- Do I want to personalize the experience? → Use a recommendation model.

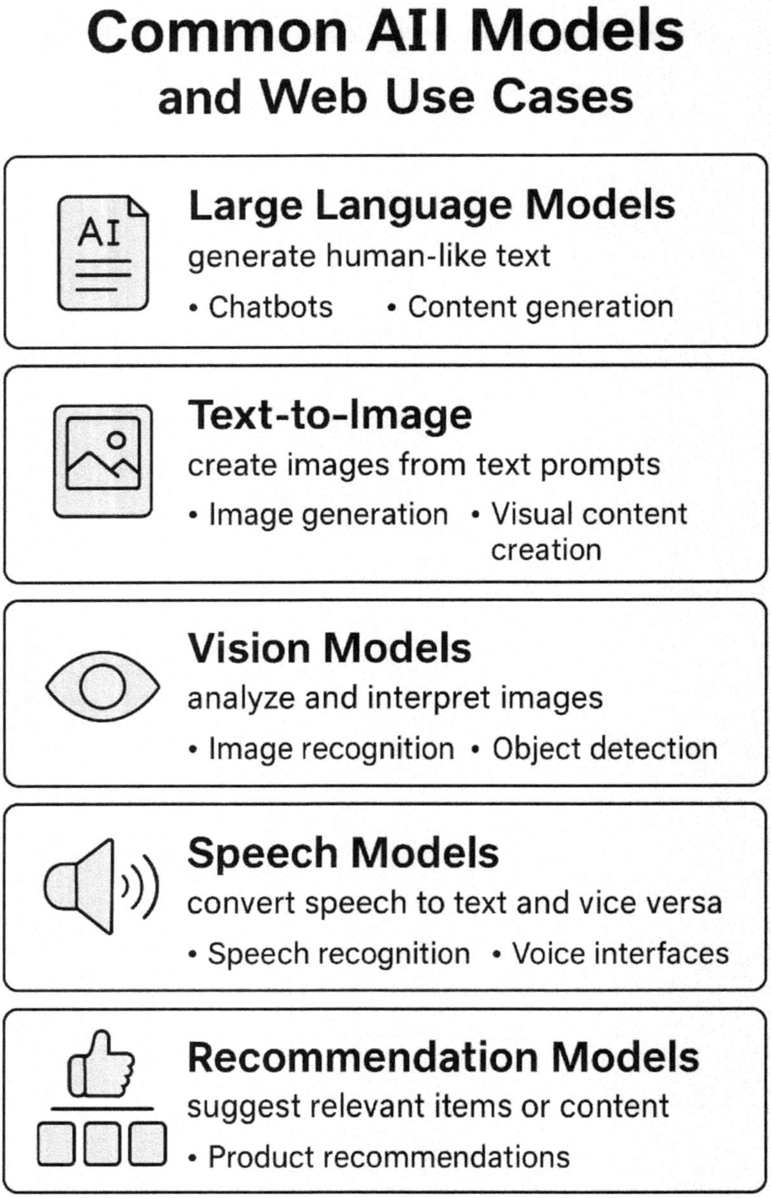
Common AI Models
and Web Use Cases
AI
Large Language Models
generate human-like text
• Chatbots
• Content generation
Text-to-Image
create images from text prompts
• Image generation
• Visual content creation
Vision Models
analyze and interpret images
• Image recognition
• Object detection
Speech Models
convert speech to text and vice versa
• Speech recognition
• Voice interfaces
Recommendation Models
suggest relevant items or content
• Product recommendations

Ethical Considerations and Best Practices

Good code is only half the story. When you add AI to a website you're also shaping how real people are profiled, nudged, or served. Below is a practical ethics checklist you can keep next to your Replit project.

1 Transparency

Tell users when, how, and ***why*** *AI is involved.*

- **Label AI features clearly** (e.g., "Powered by GPT-4").
- Provide a short, readable FAQ or tooltip that explains the model's role and major limitations.
- Log decisions: keep server-side traces of prompts/responses for audits.

2 Privacy & Data Protection

Collect the minimum, store it safely, and encrypt in transit and at rest.

- Strip PII before sending to external APIs.
- Use Replit **Secrets** for API keys and environment variables.
- Add automatic data-retention rules-e.g., delete chat logs older than 30 days.

3 Fairness & Bias Mitigation

Models inherit the biases of their training data; you inherit the responsibility.

- Run representative test prompts (different dialects, genders, cultures) and compare outputs.
- Post-filter with rule-based checks (e.g., block hateful or discriminatory language).
- Offer a feedback button so users can flag biased responses.

4 Accountability & Governance

Someone-not "the algorithm"-owns the outcome.

- Assign an internal owner for each AI feature.
- Document version numbers of every external model and the date you integrated it.
- Create rollback hooks (feature flags) so you can disable the AI path instantly if issues surface.

5 Safety & Misuse Prevention

Anticipate worst-case prompts and edge cases.

- Rate-limit sensitive endpoints to stop prompt-injection abuse.
- Sanitize user input before inserting it into prompts.
- Add moderation layers (OpenAI Moderation, Perspective API, or custom regex) to filter disallowed content.

Coding Patterns That Support Ethical AI

Pattern	Why It Helps	Quick Snippet
Server-side proxy	Hides keys, lets you scrub data before the model sees it	const safePrompt = sanitize(userPrompt); const res = await openai.chat(safePrompt);
Feature flag	Fast rollback if outputs go wrong	if (process.env.AI_ENABLED !== 'true') return fallbackResponse;
Human-in-the-loop	Critical for high-stakes	Show AI recommendation → require manual "Approve" click

Pattern	Why It Helps	Quick Snippet
	actions (billing, legal advice)	

Checklist Before You Deploy

- I've documented what data leaves the browser.
- API keys are stored in **Secrets**, not the front-end.
- I can turn off AI endpoints without redeploying.
- Users can export or delete their data.
- An abuse channel is visible (email, feedback form).

When in Doubt, Keep It Simple

If you're unsure whether an AI feature might harm, exclude, or confuse users, launch a minimal version, collect opt-in feedback, and iterate. Most ethical pitfalls come from rushing features without these guardrails.

Use the infographic above as a quick reference when you plan or review any intelligent feature in your Replit projects. Build smart-but also build responsibly.

ETHICAL AI PRINCIPLES
FOR WEB DEVELOPERS
TRANSPARENCY
PRIVACY
FAIRNESS
ACCOUNTABILITY
SAFETY
FOR WEB DEVELOPERS

Chapter 4: Integrating AI APIs

Understanding APIs and Endpoints

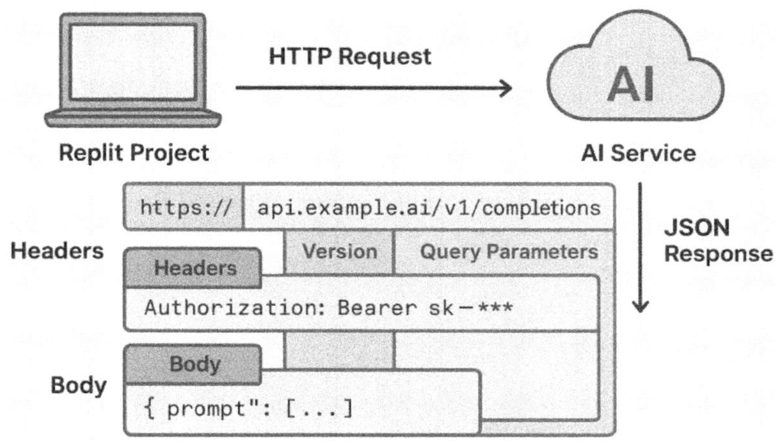

The above figure illustrates the flow of a single request from your Replit project to a cloud AI service and back.

1. What an API Really Is

An **application programming interface (API)** is just a contract. It tells your code:

- what it can ask for (the *method* and *path*),
- how to ask (the *headers* and *body*), and
- what it should expect back (status codes and response schema).

In practice, nearly every public AI service (OpenAI, Cohere, Hugging Face, Replicate) exposes a **REST-style** HTTP API. You send a

JSON payload over HTTPS and receive JSON in return. The simplicity hides a lot of power-models train for months so you can get answers in milliseconds.

2. Anatomy of an Endpoint

Piece	Example value	Why it matters
Protocol	https://	Always encrypted; browsers and Replit's outbound network block plain HTTP.
Base URL	api.openai.com	DNS name or IP of the service. Often region-specific for latency.
Version segment	/v1/	Lets providers ship breaking changes without breaking your code (until you opt-in).
Resource path	completions	Noun describing what you're operating on-models, embeddings, fine-tunes.
Query string	?user=dr-mo&stream=false	Optional filters; avoid putting secrets here-they end up in logs.
HTTP method	POST	Semantics: GET = safe read, POST = create/infer, DELETE = remove, etc.
Headers	Authorization: Bearer sk-…	Where auth lives. Also set Content-Type: application/json.

Piece	Example value	Why it matters
Body	{ "prompt": "Hello, AI" }	The request payload-often JSON, sometimes multipart for file uploads.

Tip ▸ When documentation shows a cURL example, dissect it into the columns above. You will never be surprised by an endpoint again.

3. Choosing the Right Protocol

While you'll meet GraphQL, gRPC, or WebSockets in other domains, **REST over HTTPS** dominates hosted AI because it's firewall-friendly and easy to debug with plain tools (curl, Postman, Replit's built-in HTTP tab).

4. Authentication Patterns

1. **Static API keys** - simplest, but treat them like passwords. *Store them in Replit Secrets (Secrets tab → key on left, value on right).*
2. **OAuth 2** - common when an AI service needs to act on behalf of end-users (e.g., call Google Drive + AI summarizer). You exchange a short-lived *access token* at runtime.
3. **Signed URLs / HMAC** - less common, useful for high-volume media uploads.

5. Versioning & Deprecation

AI models evolve quickly. Providers usually:

- Embed the version in the path (/v1/, /v2-alpha/) **or**
- Accept a header (OpenAI-Version: 2025-06-01).

Pin the version you develop against; schedule time to review release notes monthly so you're not forced into a breaking change the night before launch.

6. Rate Limits and Throttling

Most AI endpoints enforce per-minute or per-day quotas. Read the docs for:

- **HTTP 429 Too Many Requests** - back off exponentially.
- **Rate-Limit-Reset header** - seconds until your bucket refills.
- **Billing units** - some services price by token, not call count.

7. Error Handling Cheatsheet

Status	Meaning	Typical cause	Fix
400	Bad Request	Malformed JSON, wrong field name	Validate before sending
401	Unauthorized	Missing/invalid key	Check Replit Secret env var
403	Forbidden	Key valid but lacks scope	Enable model or grant permission
429	Too Many Requests	Exceeded rate/billing	Delay & retry w/ backoff
500	Internal Error	Provider issue	Retry, open support ticket if persistent

Log the full response body; providers often include error.code and error.message that save you hours.

8. Hands-On: Calling the OpenAI Completion Endpoint in Replit

```
import os, json, requests


API_KEY = os.getenv("OPENAI_API_KEY")        # Saved in
Secrets tab

BASE_URL = "https://api.openai.com/v1"

ENDPOINT = f"{BASE_URL}/completions"


payload = {
    "model": "gpt-4o-mini",
    "prompt": "Briefly explain API endpoints to a new dev.",
    "max_tokens": 100,
    "temperature": 0.7,
    "user": "dr-mo"                      # Helps provider trace abuse
}


headers = {
    "Authorization": f"Bearer {API_KEY}",
    "Content-Type": "application/json"
}


response = requests.post(ENDPOINT, headers=headers,
json=payload, timeout=30)

response.raise_for_status()            # Raises on 4xx/5xx
```

print(json.dumps(response.json(), indent=2))

Why this works on Replit

- The outbound firewall allows HTTPS by default-no extra config.
- Secret keys never show up in the public workspace if you use Secrets.
- The requests library is pre-installed in most Python templates; otherwise poetry add requests.

9. Discoverability & Self-Documentation

- **OpenAPI/Swagger JSON** - many AI vendors expose it at /docs or /openapi.json; import into Postman or Replit's HTTP client for auto-generated explorers.
- **Postman collections** - quicker for one-off tests.
- **SDK generators** - point them at OpenAPI, get typed clients in Python/TS.

10. Key Takeaways

- An endpoint is a URL-plus-method, nothing mystical.
- Keep secrets out of code; use Replit Secrets.
- Pin versions, respect rate limits, parse error bodies.
- Treat the docs as contracts-but verify them with live calls early.

You're now ready to wire any AI service into your web app. In the next section we'll build a *serverless* route on Replit that proxies user input to your chosen model and streams results back in real time.

Popular AI API Providers

To build intelligent features into your Replit web apps-like chatbots, summarizers, image generators, or language translators-you'll often reach for APIs provided by leading AI model platforms. This section introduces the most commonly used providers, how they differ, and when to use each.

1. OpenAI

Strengths: High-quality general-purpose models (GPT-4o, DALL·E 3, Whisper), strong documentation, robust infrastructure.
Use Cases: Chatbots, coding assistants, content generation, audio transcription, vision + language.
API Style: REST over HTTPS.
Authentication: Bearer token via secret key.
Pricing: Pay-as-you-go, with tiered usage rates per model and modality. No long-term commitment required.
Popular Endpoints:

- /v1/completions - GPT-3.5 and GPT-4 (text completion)
- /v1/chat/completions - GPT chat-style interaction
- /v1/images/generations - DALL·E
- /v1/audio/transcriptions - Whisper

Best for: When you need top-tier performance and multimodal capabilities in one unified platform.

2. Hugging Face

Strengths: Home to 300,000+ models, including both hosted APIs and downloadable open-source models. Community-driven with transparency.
Use Cases: Custom model deployment, language modeling, translation, embeddings, audio processing.
API Style: Hosted Inference API (REST), and Spaces for UI demos.

Authentication: API token in headers.
Pricing: Free for public models with limits; paid tiers offer higher throughput and private hosting.
Popular Models:

- sentence-transformers/all-MiniLM-L6-v2 - for sentence embeddings
- bigscience/bloom - open-access LLM
- Salesforce/blip-image-captioning-base - vision-language tasks

Best for: Developers wanting flexibility, transparency, and access to niche or experimental models.

3. Cohere

Strengths: Optimized for enterprise NLP tasks like embeddings, classification, and summarization. Multilingual and fast.
Use Cases: Semantic search, chat interfaces, business document processing.
API Style: RESTful JSON-based API.
Authentication: Bearer token.
Pricing: Free tier during beta; usage-based after.
Popular Endpoints:

- /v1/generate - text generation
- /v1/embed - sentence and document embeddings
- /v1/classify - zero/few-shot classification

Best for: Search, semantic understanding, and structured NLP tasks.

4. Replicate

Strengths: API wrapper for running models in containers, typically open-source. It hosts models that require GPU and are often too heavy to run client-side.
Use Cases: Art generation, video interpolation, face enhancement,

music generation, LLMs like LLaMA and SDXL.
API Style: REST, but often involves asynchronous polling (due to long-running inference).
Authentication: Token in headers.
Pricing: Usage-based; billed per second of inference time.
Popular Models:

- stability-ai/stable-diffusion - text-to-image
- meta-llama/Llama-3-70b - open LLM
- riffusion/riffusion - music from text

Best for: Running large open-source models with GPU needs and getting quick access to the bleeding edge.

5. Anthropic

Strengths: Safety-focused LLMs (Claude 3 family), long context windows, helpful for assistant-style use.
Use Cases: Chatbots, summarization, ideation, safe content generation.
API Style: Chat-based; similar to OpenAI's Chat Completions API.
Authentication: Bearer token.
Pricing: Token-based, competitive with OpenAI.
Popular Models:

- claude-3-opus - top-tier
- claude-3-sonnet - balance of speed and power
- claude-3-haiku - fastest and cheapest

Best for: Use cases requiring long inputs (like full PDFs or transcripts) and strong alignment out of the box.

6. Google Vertex AI / PaLM / Gemini

Strengths: Tight integration with Google Cloud, large model family, good for enterprises already using GCP.

Use Cases: Enterprise AI, document understanding, structured tool integration.
API Style: REST + client SDKs.
Authentication: OAuth 2 with service accounts.
Pricing: Pay-as-you-go with quotas via GCP.
Popular Models:

- Gemini 1.5 Pro - multimodal with long context
- PaLM 2 - earlier large language models

Best for: Enterprise-grade apps with existing GCP setup.

Quick Comparison Table

Provider	**Strengths**	**Best For**	**Free Tier**	**Notable Model**
OpenAI	Quality, multimodal, reliability	Production-ready apps	Limited	GPT-4o
Hugging Face	Model variety, openness	Custom or experimental work	Yes	Bloom, T5
Cohere	Embeddings, multilingual NLP	Semantic tasks	Yes (beta)	Embed v3
Replicate	Open-source GPU model access	Creative tools, vision	No	SDXL, LLaMA
Anthropic	Long context, aligned responses	Assistants, summarizers	Limited	Claude 3

Provider	Strengths	Best For	Free Tier	Notable Model
Google	Enterprise integration	Structured business AI	With GCP	Gemini 1.5 Pro

Summary

Choosing the right API provider depends on the task at hand. OpenAI is a solid default, but Hugging Face and Replicate offer unmatched flexibility and community insight. Cohere shines in language-centric workflows, while Anthropic and Google focus on safety and enterprise scale.

In the next section, we'll walk through how to set up a Replit project to consume any of these APIs using environment secrets and Python or Node.js-so you're not locked into a single ecosystem.

AI API Provider Landscape 2025
OpenAI
• High-quality models
• Chatbots, code gen
• Limited free tier
Hugging Face
• Model variety & openness
• Pue tier use cases
Replicate
• Open-source models
• Creative tools, vision
• No free tier
Anthropic
• Aligned language models
• Assistants, summarizers
Replicate
• Open-source models
• Creative tools, vision
• No free tier
Google
• Enterprise integration
• Structured apps
• With Google Cloud

Setting Up Environment Variables in Replit

Th figure below shows the Secrets panel and a Python snippet side-by-side. The arrow makes it clear that os.getenv("OPENAI_API_KEY") pulls from the value you store in the UI.

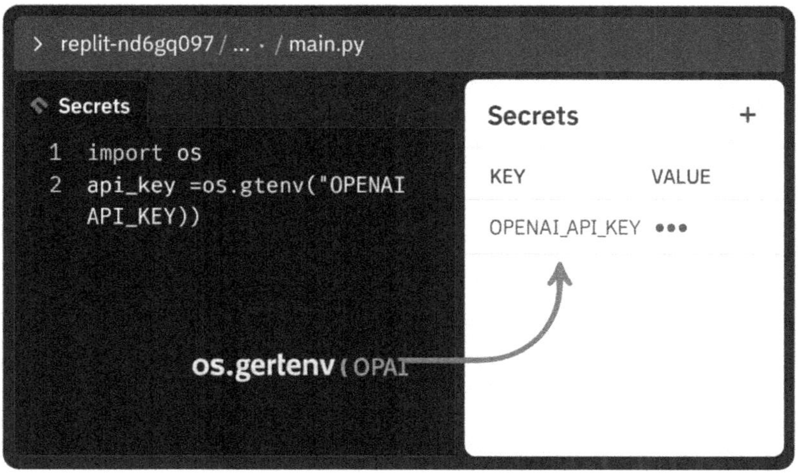

1. Why Use Environment Variables?

Hard-coding keys in source files is a security risk-anyone who forks your Repl or browses your public Git history could steal them. Environment variables keep credentials in a separate, private store that:

- never appears in your git commits,
- is encrypted at rest by Replit,
- can be rotated without touching code, and
- works the same in Python, Node.js, Go, or Bash.

2. Adding a Secret in Replit

1. **Open the *Secrets* panel**
   Click the padlock icon (right-hand toolbar).
2. **Create a key–value pair**
   Key → OPENAI_API_KEY
   Value → paste the real key from your provider's dashboard.
3. **Save**
   Replit masks the value with •••. It's accessible to your code at runtime but hidden in the editor and logs.

3. Accessing Secrets in Code

Language	Sample code
Python	python\nimport os\napi_key = os.getenv(\"OPENAI_API_KEY\")\n
Node.js	js\nimport 'dotenv/config';\nconst apiKey = process.env.OPENAI_API_KEY;\n
Go	go\napiKey := os.Getenv(\"OPENAI_API_KEY\")\n

For Node.js, Replit automatically injects variables into process.env; you don't need a .env file locally but adding dotenv keeps parity with local development.

4. Local Development vs. Replit Cloud

Context	Where variables live	How to create them
Replit IDE	Secrets tab (server-side store)	UI input; never added to repo

Context	Where variables live	How to create them
Local machine	.env file in project root	Add to .gitignore, load with dotenv or your shell
CI/CD (GitHub Actions, etc.)	Encrypted project secrets	Set in repo or org settings

Keep variable *names* identical across environments so your code stays portable.

5. Rotating Keys Safely

1. Generate a new key in the provider dashboard.
2. Add the new value to Replit Secrets alongside the old one (e.g., OPENAI_API_KEY_NEW).
3. Deploy, verify, then remove the old key and update the variable back to the canonical name.

This zero-downtime pattern avoids breaking live traffic.

6. Scoped & Project-Specific Keys

Some providers let you create multiple keys with limited scopes (e.g., "read-only embeddings" vs. "full model access"). Use the minimal scope required:

```
# Example policy for OpenAI fine-tunes (conceptual)

permissions:

  - read:embeddings

  - write:chat.completions
```

Store each key under a descriptive env var (HF_READ_TOKEN, REPLICATE_MODEL_RUNNER) so teammates know what it's for.

7. Secrets in Forks & Template Repls

When someone **forks** your Repl:

- the code copies over,
- Secrets do **not**.

That means examples stay runnable-but people must add their own keys. Add a README.md line:

1. Click 🔒 **Secrets**

2. Add `OPENAI_API_KEY` with your own token

8. Debugging "Key Not Found" Errors

- In Python, print os.environ.keys() to confirm the var is injected.
- Ensure you restarted the Repl after adding a new Secret-Replit refreshes env only on run.
- Watch for typos: OPENAI_API_KEY ≠ OPENAI_KEY.

9. Key Takeaways

- Use the Secrets tab for anything you wouldn't post publicly.
- Access values through standard env APIs (os.getenv, process.env).
- Mirror names across local, cloud, and CI for hassle-free moves.
- Rotate keys with overlap to avoid downtime.

Your Replit workspace is now ready to call any AI provider securely.

Making API Requests from Your Website

The figure below shows a typical flow: the browser calls your Replit-hosted route (/api/chat), the route proxies to the AI provider, and streams the response back to the UI.

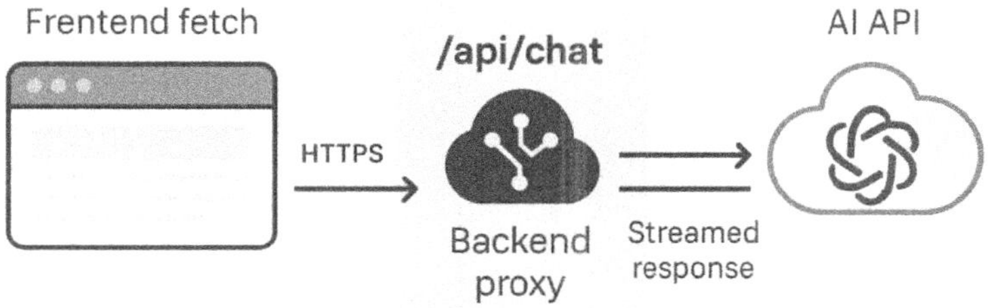

1. Front End vs. Back End Calls

Approach	Pros	Cons	When to choose
Direct from browser (fetching the AI endpoint)	Simplest code; no server required	Exposes your key to users; CORS limits; harder to stream	Almost never-use only with public, key-free endpoints
Proxy through your server (recommended)	Keeps keys secret; adds caching, rate-	One extra hop; need to write a few	Nearly always for paid AI services

Approach	Pros	Cons	When to choose
	limit handling, and model–agnostic logic	lines of server code	

---

2. Building the Proxy Route in Replit (Node + Express)

```
// server.js  (run with `node server.js`)
import express from "express";
import fetch from "node-fetch";
import cors from "cors";

const app = express();
app.use(cors());
app.use(express.json());

app.post("/api/chat", async (req, res) => {
  const { messages } = req.body;      // [{role, content}, ...]
  try {
    const upstream = await
fetch("https://api.openai.com/v1/chat/completions", {
      method: "POST",
      headers: {
```

```
      "Content-Type": "application/json",
      "Authorization": `Bearer ${process.env.OPENAI_API_KEY}`,
    },
    body: JSON.stringify({
      model: "gpt-4o-mini",
      stream: true,
      messages,
    }),
  });

  // Forward the streaming chunks unmodified
  res.setHeader("Content-Type", "text/event-stream");
  for await (const chunk of upstream.body) res.write(chunk);
  res.end();
 } catch (err) {
  console.error(err);
  res.status(502).json({ error: "Upstream AI request failed" });
 }
});

app.listen(3000, () => console.log("API proxy on
http://localhost:3000"));
```

Why stream?

Users see words appear gradually, latency feels lower, and you pay only for tokens generated so far if a user cancels mid-response.

3. Calling the Proxy from the Browser

```
// chat.js (client side)

export async function askChat(messages, onToken) {

  const resp = await fetch("/api/chat", {

    method: "POST",

    headers: { "Content-Type": "application/json" },

    body: JSON.stringify({ messages }),

  });


  const reader = resp.body.getReader();

  const decoder = new TextDecoder("utf-8");

  let buffer = "";


  while (true) {

    const { done, value } = await reader.read();

    if (done) break;

    buffer += decoder.decode(value, { stream: true });

    const tokens = buffer.split("\n");

    buffer = tokens.pop();          // keep last partial

    tokens.forEach(onToken);          // callback for each token
```

```
  }
}
```

Hook this into a React state update to paint words to the screen as they arrive.

4. Guard Rails in Production

1. **Rate Limiting** – Use express-rate-limit or Cloudflare Workers KV to cap requests per IP.
2. **Schema Validation** – Validate req.body with Zod or Joi before forwarding.
3. **Timeouts & Retries** – Set fetch's signal with AbortController; retry idempotent calls with exponential back-off.
4. **Caching** – Cache embeddings or expensive prompts in Redis for repeat queries.
5. **Logging** – Log the prompt footprint (token count, user ID) but never raw PII.

5. Handling Large Files

For vision or speech endpoints that require multipart uploads:

```
const form = new FormData();

form.append("file", selectedFile);

form.append("model", "whisper-large");

fetch("/api/transcribe", { method: "POST", body: form });
```

Backend route: stream the multipart body directly to the provider to avoid loading the entire file in memory.

6. Cross-Origin Front Ends

If your front end is hosted on a separate origin (e.g., Vercel or Netlify):

```
app.use(cors({
  origin: ["https://my-frontend.vercel.app"],
  methods: ["POST"],
  maxAge: 86400
}));
```

Keep the proxy in the same Repl to avoid CORS headaches during development.

7. Debugging Checklist

Symptom	Likely cause	Fix
401 Unauthorized	Wrong or missing key	Check process.env, rotate key
CORS error in console	Fetching AI provider directly	Use proxy or adjust headers
Empty response / connection reset	Stream aborted early	Increase timeout, check provider status
High latency	Model load-time or poor region match	Try smaller model or region-specific endpoint

8. Key Takeaways

- Send browser requests to **your backend**; never expose secrets client-side.

- Stream responses for chat-like UX.
- Protect your route with rate limits and validation.
- The same proxy pattern works for image, audio, and embedding endpoints.

You now have a battle-tested recipe for calling any AI API from a Replit-hosted web app.

Handling API Responses and Errors

Even with a well-formed request and a valid API key, things can still go wrong. Maybe the user hits your endpoint too quickly, the API provider is down, or the payload exceeds token limits. That's why robust error handling is a must-not only for a better user experience, but also to avoid unexpected bugs, wasted compute costs, and hard-to-debug failures.

1. Understanding AI API Responses

Most modern AI APIs (like OpenAI, Cohere, or Hugging Face) return data in a standard JSON format. On success, you'll get structured results. On failure, you'll typically get something like this:

```
{
  "error": {
    "message": "You exceeded your current quota. Please check your plan and billing details.",
    "type": "insufficient_quota",
    "param": null,
    "code": "insufficient_quota"
  }
}
```

Check both the **HTTP status code** and the **error body**. The code gives a high-level summary (e.g., 401, 429, 500), while the error object usually contains human-readable and machine-parsable info.

2. Key HTTP Status Codes to Handle

Status Code	Meaning	Action to Take
200	OK	✅ Proceed normally
400	Bad Request	🛠 Fix the request body or parameters
401	Unauthorized	🔑 Check API key, scope, or token
403	Forbidden	🔒 Key valid, but lacks permission
429	Too Many Requests	⏱ Back off, implement rate limiting
500	Internal Server Error	🔁 Retry after short delay
503	Service Unavailable	📉 Retry with backoff, maybe alert

Use response.ok in JavaScript or response.raise_for_status() in Python to handle these cases consistently.

3. Implementing Safe Error Handling (Node.js example)

```
// Inside your API route
try {
  const res = await
fetch("https://api.openai.com/v1/chat/completions", {
    method: "POST",
    headers: {
      "Authorization": `Bearer ${process.env.OPENAI_API_KEY}`,
      "Content-Type": "application/json"
    },
    body: JSON.stringify(payload)
  });

  if (!res.ok) {
    const errorData = await res.json();
    console.error("AI Error:", errorData);
    return res.status(res.status).json({ error: errorData.error.message
});
  }

  const data = await res.json();
  return res.json(data);
```

```
} catch (err) {
  console.error("Unexpected error:", err.message);
  return res.status(500).json({ error: "AI service unreachable or failed." });
}
```

4. Retry Logic: When and How

Some errors are transient-you can safely retry them after a short delay. Others are permanent, and retrying just wastes time.

Error Type	Retry?	Strategy
Quota exhausted	❌	Tell user to upgrade account
Temporary service issue	✅	Retry with exponential backoff
Network timeout	✅	Retry a few times, then fail
Invalid API key	❌	Show configuration instructions
Payload too large	❌	Validate before sending

Use libraries like axios-retry (Node.js) or tenacity (Python) to make retries clean and configurable.

5. Providing Meaningful Feedback to Users

Don't just fail silently or dump raw errors. Instead, provide helpful, user-readable messages:

```
// In the frontend
try {
  const res = await fetch("/api/chat", { method: "POST", body: ... });
```

```
  const data = await res.json();
  if (!res.ok) throw new Error(data.error);
  render(data.response);
} catch (err) {
  showToast("Something went wrong: " + err.message);
}
```

If you're calling a streaming endpoint, remember: once a stream starts, it's harder to send structured error info. Always validate your request and check quotas before starting a stream.

6. Defensive Programming Tips

- **Always check response.ok** before parsing body JSON.
- **Validate payloads** before sending them to the provider.
- **Log errors with context**: include the user ID (if available), prompt size, model used, and time.
- **Rate limit user input** with a delay or debounce so you don't hammer your quota.

7. Logging and Observability

Track these metrics:

- Success/failure rate per endpoint
- Avg. latency per provider
- Frequent error types (like rate_limit_exceeded)
- Which prompts tend to fail

You can use Replit's built-in logging or connect to a third-party service like Logtail, Sentry, or Supabase logs.

Handling API Responses and Errors

i. **AI APl Response Format** Figure 5-1 sigures a typical error response from OpenAls chat completion API

```
{ "error": "You exceeded your curremt quota, please
     check your plan and Bitling
   "type". "insufficient_qubta",
   "param": "aull",
   'code": "insufficient_quota"
}
```

Figre-5-1-1 Example error respon se from OpenAl scaple

2. **Checking HTTP Status Codes:** Use the ok property for statuses outside a 2xx x range, ensures parsing doesn't fail silently when body is empty

```
fetch(/apl/chat. {
  method. "POsT"
  headers: ( " (Content-Type)."application/json"),
  body, .$: atlrt(fyttes_message .))
  .then(psvmer (response &4-b)
   consal csa = ova:{ responsetext(): safely save empty body
   lT  :response_dk),redurn data
   throw new Frror(data error—message)
   setError(Try falled (attempt//3)-$: Serror, message)
  }
}
```

3. **Using Try/Catch:** Wrap-asyrcho code that could throw the async, parsers, es, fetch', to prevent ignored errors from hanging spinner.
4. **Error Handling Example:** Integrates Try/Catch, a user teedback loop, a retry pattern.
6. **Providing User Feedback:** Provide specific, actionable messages to help users self-diagnose-and recover. Use raw error 'messages.
6. **Non-Retriable Quota Errors:** Avoid wasteful retries for foreeseible errors like example in Eigute 5-1 as they are not self-recovering.

Summary

Error handling in AI apps isn't just about preventing crashes-it's about building trust and clarity into your experience. Whether you're summarizing documents or powering a chat assistant, your users will appreciate transparency when something breaks.

Checklist for each AI call:

- ✅ Check HTTP status
- ✅ Handle error fields in body
- ✅ Retry only if it makes sense
- ✅ Show actionable feedback to user
- ✅ Log everything for later diagnosis

Chapter 5: Building Your First AI-Powered Website

Project Overview - AI Chatbot

For your first full project, we're going to build something practical, popular, and easy to expand on: a simple **AI-powered chatbot**. This app will serve as your gateway into dynamic, real-time interactions with powerful language models via API.

This section provides a complete overview of what you'll build, what tools are involved, and how the pieces connect inside Replit.

1. What You're Building

A basic, responsive website where a user can type a message and receive a reply from an AI model (such as GPT-4o or Cohere's Command R+). We'll include:

- A text input for user messages
- A conversation history log
- A Replit-hosted backend route that sends each message to an AI API
- Streaming responses from the API (so replies feel fast and interactive)

2. Key Features

Feature	Description
Live chat UI	Powered by HTML, CSS, and JavaScript (or a front-end framework like React if desired)
Backend proxy	Handles API requests and keeps your API key hidden from users

Feature	Description
Environment secrets	Store your API key securely in Replit
Streaming response	Words appear as they're generated by the model
Model flexibility	Can plug in OpenAI, Hugging Face, Cohere, etc.
Serverless deploy	All runs from a single Replit workspace

3. Tech Stack

Layer	Tool
Frontend	HTML, CSS, JS (or React)
Backend	Node.js (Express) or Python (Flask/FastAPI)
AI API	OpenAI, Cohere, or Hugging Face
Hosting	Replit's built-in web server
Secrets	Replit Secrets tab (API keys)

We'll use the Node.js stack in this walkthrough, but a Python version is easy to swap in.

4. Architecture Overview

See the diagram below for how the pieces fit together.

- The browser sends a message to the backend using fetch()

- The backend route /api/chat proxies the request to the AI provider
- The AI returns a response (ideally streamed)
- The frontend renders the response token by token

5. Design Goals

This project is intentionally minimal. The goal is not to ship a production-grade chatbot, but to learn:

- How to securely call an AI API
- How to handle asynchronous interaction (e.g., streaming)
- How to build a UI around a real-time AI experience
- How to debug and extend each layer

Later chapters will build on this to add user accounts, input validation, prompt design, and fine-tuned models.

6. What You'll Learn

By the end of this project, you'll be able to:

✅ Set up secure API routes in Replit
✅ Connect a frontend input to a backend call
✅ Stream and display model responses
✅ Handle user errors and edge cases
✅ Use Secrets and environment variables effectively
✅ Plug in different model providers with minimal change

7. Project Preview (Before You Build)

Here's what your final chatbot will look like in the browser:

💬 *User*: How do I write a good prompt?

🤖 *AI*: Writing a good prompt involves clarity, specificity, and intent...

You'll see new messages stream in, not just appear all at once.

8. Diagram: Chatbot Architecture

The figure below shows the flow of data from browser input to AI API and back

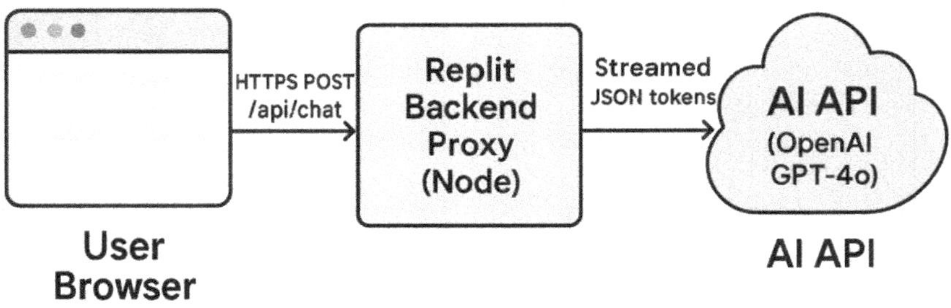

Diagram Key:

- Left: Browser with input box
- Center: Replit server route /api/chat
- Right: Cloud-hosted AI model (e.g., GPT-4)
- Arrows: Request flow (left to right), Streamed response (right to left)

Designing the User Interface

A chatbot lives or dies by how comfortable it feels to type into-and how quickly it replies. Let's break down the UI elements you need and the decisions behind them.

1. Layout at a Glance

The figure below shows a wireframe of the final chat panel.

- **Header**
  A single-line title ("Chat") keeps things obvious without wasting vertical space.
- **Chat history container**
  A flex column that scrolls. Use overflow-y: auto so long answers don't push the input off-screen.
- **Message bubbles**
  Different background shades for user and AI. Keep rounded corners moderate (6-8 px) to fit both mobile and desktop.
- **Typing indicator**
  A lightweight "Generating response…" line that appears while you stream tokens.
- **Input row**
  A text field that expands on focus, plus a send button with an arrow icon. Add enterKeyHint="send" on mobile for a nicer keyboard.

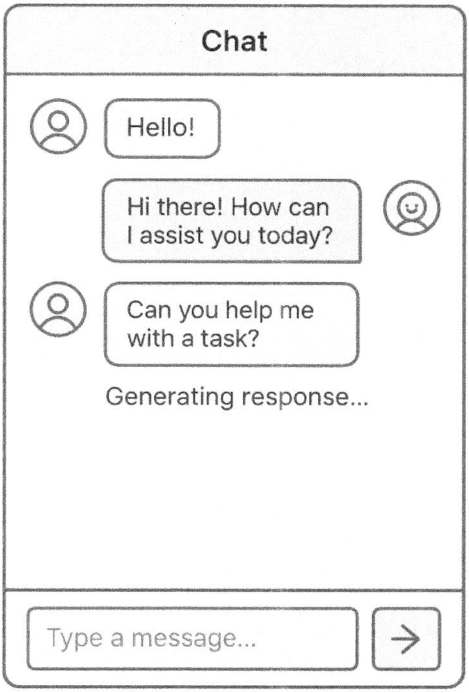

2. Responsive Rules

Breakpoint	Change
max-width: 600px	Input row snaps to 100 %, bubbles shrink to 90 % width
min-width: 601px	Max bubble width 70 %, adds subtle shadow
prefers-color-scheme: dark	Swap light gray bubbles for charcoal / slate tones

Use CSS Grid for the page skeleton and flexbox for the chat column. It avoids media-query overload.

3. Accessibility Checklist

1. **Contrast** – 4.5:1 for text in bubbles.
2. **Keyboard nav** – Tab cycles: input → send → last message.
3. **ARIA roles** – role="log" on the chat container, aria-live="polite" on the typing indicator.
4. **Motion** – Keep animations under 100 ms, respect prefers-reduced-motion.

4. Streaming-Friendly Rendering

While tokens stream from the backend you'll re-render fast. In React:

```
function ChatBubble({ content, from }) {
  return (
    <div className={from === 'user' ? 'bubble user' : 'bubble ai'}>
      {content}
    </div>
  );
}


function ChatWindow() {
  const [messages, setMessages] = useState([]);
  const [draft, setDraft] = useState('');
  const [loading, setLoading] = useState(false);
```

```
  async function send() {
    setLoading(true);
    const stream = fetch('/api/chat', { ... }).then(r =>
r.body.getReader());
    let buffer = '';
    while (true) {
      const { done, value } = await stream.read();
      if (done) break;
      buffer += new TextDecoder().decode(value, { stream: true });
      setMessages(prev => [...prev.slice(0, -1), { from: 'ai', content:
buffer }]);
    }
    setLoading(false);
  }
  ...
}
```

5. Styling Snippets (vanilla CSS)

```
.chat-container { display: flex; flex-direction: column; height: 100vh;
}
.history { flex: 1 1 auto; padding: 1rem; overflow-y: auto; }
.bubble { padding: .75rem 1rem; margin: .25rem 0; border-radius:
8px; line-height: 1.4; }
.user { background: #e8f0fe; align-self: flex-end; }
```

.ai { background: #f1f3f4; align-self: flex-start; }

.input-row { display: flex; gap: .5rem; padding: .75rem; border-top: 1px solid #ddd; }

input[type="text"] { flex: 1; padding: .6rem .75rem; border: 1px solid #ccc; border-radius: 6px; }

button.send { width: 3rem; border: none; border-radius: 6px; background: #3b82f6; color:#fff; }

6. Extending the UI Later

- **Avatar icons** for user/AI to humanize conversation
- **Markdown rendering** (react-markdown) for rich answers
- **Copy-to-clipboard** on code blocks
- **Attachments panel** for image or file inputs (vision models)

Design with headroom so new widgets slot in without a full redesign.

Connecting the Frontend to the Backend

A chat UI is only half the story. Now we'll wire the browser's **fetch** call to the /api/chat proxy you built earlier, handle streamed tokens, and surface errors.

1. End-to-End Flow

The figure below visualizes the four-step round-trip.

1. **ChatInput.js** sends a POST request to /api/chat.
2. The backend relays the JSON body to the AI provider.
3. The provider streams tokens back.
4. **ChatWindow** appends tokens to the conversation.

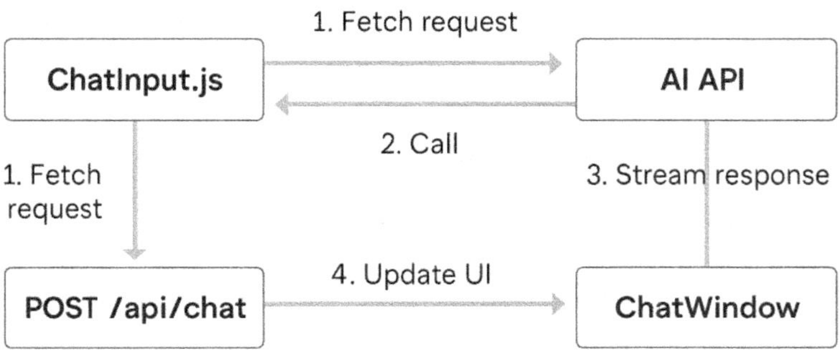

2. Frontend Fetch Helper (React)

```
export async function streamChat(messages, onToken) {
  const res = await fetch("/api/chat", {
    method: "POST",
    headers: { "Content-Type": "application/json" },
    body: JSON.stringify({ messages }),
  });
  if (!res.ok) throw new Error(await res.text());

  const reader = res.body.getReader();
  const decoder = new TextDecoder("utf-8");
  let buffer = "";
```

```
 while (true) {
  const { done, value } = await reader.read();
  if (done) break;
  buffer += decoder.decode(value, { stream: true });

  // tokens are separated by newline
  const parts = buffer.split("\n");
  buffer = parts.pop();        // keep last partial
  parts.forEach(onToken);      // push full tokens up
 }
}
```

3. Integrating with ChatWindow State

```
function ChatWindow() {
 const [msgs, setMsgs] = useState([]);
 const [draft, setDraft] = useState("");
 const [loading, setLoading] = useState(false);

 async function send() {
  const next = [...msgs, { from: "user", content: draft }];
  setMsgs(next);
  setDraft("");
```

```
    setLoading(true);

    // reserve a placeholder for the AI reply
    setMsgs(m => [...m, { from: "ai", content: "" }]);

    try {
      await streamChat(next, token =>
        setMsgs(m => {
          const copy = [...m];
          copy[copy.length - 1].content += token;
          return copy;
        })
      );
    } finally {
      setLoading(false);
    }
  }
  ...
}
```

Key idea: stream handler updates only the last AI bubble, giving a typewriter effect with almost zero re-renders.

4. Backend Route Recap (Node/Express)

```
app.post("/api/chat", async (req, res) => {
  const upstream = await
fetch("https://api.openai.com/v1/chat/completions", {
    method: "POST",
    headers: {
      "Authorization": `Bearer ${process.env.OPENAI_API_KEY}`,
      "Content-Type": "application/json",
    },
    body: JSON.stringify({
      model: "gpt-4o-mini",
      stream: true,
      messages: req.body.messages,
    }),
  });

  res.setHeader("Content-Type", "text/event-stream"); // SSE
  for await (const chunk of upstream.body) res.write(chunk);
  res.end();
});
```

SSE (text/event-stream) keeps things simple: no WebSockets, no polling - just one long-lived HTTP response.

5. CORS & Same-Origin Tips

If your frontend and backend live in the same Replit, fetch("/api/chat") works out of the box.
Hosting the UI elsewhere? Add:

app.use(cors({ origin: "https://your-frontend.com", methods: ["POST"] }));

6. Error Paths to Cover

Failure point	Symptom in browser	Fix
401/403 from provider	Immediate JSON with "error"	Rotate API key, check scope
429 rate limit	Stream never starts	Show cooldown timer, retry later
Network drop mid-stream	Reader throws	Re-request last 3 messages

Provide user-friendly fallbacks - "Hmm, I'm overloaded, try again in a sec" - instead of raw stack traces.

7. Going Further

- **AbortController** to cancel a long reply when the user sends a new question.
- **Message IDs** so the backend can resume streams if the connection drops.
- **WebSockets** if you need bi-directional events (e.g., typing indicators from both sides).

With the data pipeline now fully connected, typing in the browser will trigger tokens from the model in real time.

Deploying and Testing Your AI Website

1. Prepare the workspace

- **Port binding** – Replit publishes whatever your app listens to on port 3000.
- **Production env vars** – Add a second secret, e.g. OPENAI_API_KEY_PROD, so you can swap keys with an if (process.env.NODE_ENV === "production") guard.
- **Start script** – In package.json, define

```
"scripts": {
  "start": "node server.js",
  "test": "vitest run"
}
```

2. Run pre-flight tests

Layer	Tool	What to test
Unit	Vitest / Jest	Utility functions, prompt builders
Integration	Supertest	/api/chat returns 200, streams tokens
UI	Playwright	Typing shows bubbles, loader disappears

Trigger them locally with npm test; green tests give you confidence before the push.

3. Deploy with Replit's "Deploy" tab

1. Click **Deploy → Create Deployment**.
2. Choose **Web App** (static + server).
3. Pick the target branch (usually main) and hit **Deploy**.

4. Replit spins a container, installs dependencies, runs npm start, and exposes an HTTPS URL such as https://chatbot.dr-mo.repl.co.

The figure below shows this pipeline from workspace to live site.

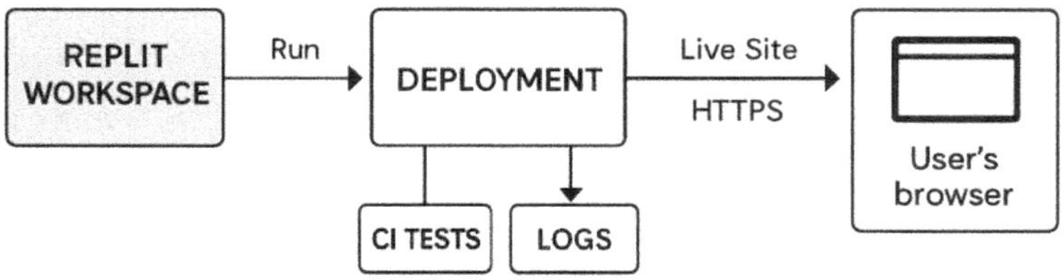

4. Smoke-test the live build

```
curl -X POST https://chatbot.dr-mo.repl.co/api/chat \
  -H "Content-Type: application/json" \
  -d '{"messages":[{"role":"user","content":"Hello"}]}'
```

You should see streamed JSON chunks. Visit the URL in a private browser window to confirm CORS and cookies behave.

5. Monitor and iterate

- **Logs** – Deploy → Logs surfaces stdout/stderr; tail them while you chat.

- **Metrics** – Watch memory and CPU graphs; GPT streaming is light, but image models are heavy.
- **Error alerts** – Add a simple Slack webhook in the catch-all error handler so you know when 500s spike.

6. Common pitfalls

Symptom	Likely cause	Fix
Deployment freezes on build	Missing node engine version	Add "engines": { "node": ">=20" }
API 401 in production only	Wrong env var name	Double-check Secrets tab
Messages hang mid-reply	Proxy times out (default 30 s)	app.post(..., { timeout: 0 }) or chunk results

7. Blue-green updates

Create a second deployment ("v2"). Run integration tests against its URL; if they pass, flip DNS by promoting v2. Zero downtime, instant rollback.

8. Checklist before sharing the link

- ✅ Tests green
- ✅ Secrets set (no dev keys)
- ✅ CORS locked to your domain
- ✅ Logs show zero errors under light load

Once everything is green, drop the URL to friends and watch the conversations roll in. Continuous improvement starts with real users

- and solid deployment & testing makes sure their first impression is flawless.

Chapter 6: Advanced AI Features

Implementing NLP

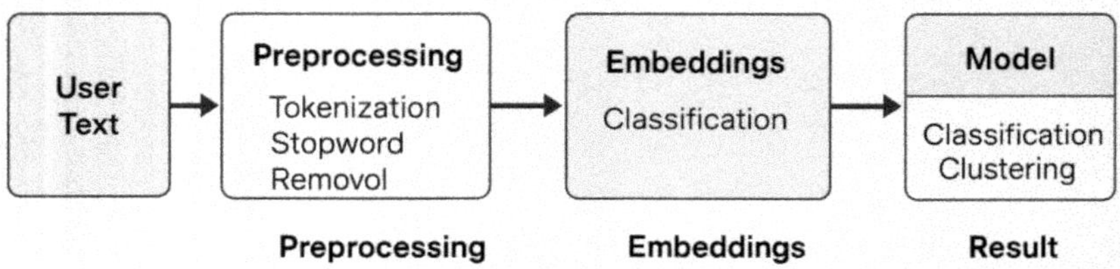

Core Pipeline (see figure)

1. **User Text** → raw string from a form, file upload, or webhook
2. **Pre-processing** → tokenization, lower-casing, stop-word removal, language-detect
3. **Embeddings** → vector representation from a hosted model (e.g., text-embedding-3-small)
4. **Model** → classifier, summarizer, or semantic search that consumes those vectors
5. **Response** → structured JSON you render back to the UI

The diagram above walks left-to-right through those stages.

Quick-Start with Hugging Face + Python

```
from transformers import pipeline

import os


os.environ["HF_TOKEN"] = os.getenv("HF_API_KEY")  # Replit
secret


classifier = pipeline(

    "text-classification",

    model="distilbert-base-uncased-finetuned-sst-2-english",

    token=os.environ["HF_TOKEN"]

)


def sentiment(text: str) -> dict:

    return classifier(text, truncation=True, max_length=256)[0]
```

Drop this in routes/sentiment.py; POST JSON { "text": "I love Replit!" } and return the label + score.

Using OpenAI Embeddings for Semantic Search

1. **Create vectors**

```
import openai, json, os, sqlite3


openai.api_key = os.getenv("OPENAI_API_KEY")

conn = sqlite3.connect("embeds.db")
```

```
conn.execute("CREATE TABLE IF NOT EXISTS docs(id INTEGER PRIMARY KEY, text, vec BLOB)")


def add_doc(text):
    vec = openai.embeddings.create(
        model="text-embedding-3-small", input=text
    ).data[0].embedding
    conn.execute("INSERT INTO docs(text, vec) VALUES(?, ?)", (text, json.dumps(vec)))
    conn.commit()
```

2. **Query**

```
import numpy as np


def search(query, k=3):
    q_vec = openai.embeddings.create(
        model="text-embedding-3-small", input=query
    ).data[0].embedding
    rows = conn.execute("SELECT text, vec FROM docs").fetchall()

    scored = [
        (text, np.dot(np.array(json.loads(vec)), q_vec)) for text, vec in rows
    ]
```

```
return sorted(scored, key=lambda x: -x[1])[:k]
```

Return the top passages to GPT-4o for a final answer ("RAG" pattern).

Real-Time Language Detection in the Frontend

```
import franc from "franc";

function detectLang(text) {

  const code = franc(text);          // e.g., 'spa'

  const lang = new Intl.DisplayNames(['en'], { type: 'language' }).of(code);

  return lang || 'Unknown';

}
```

Show a flag next to each message so users know the bot recognized their language.

Handling Large Inputs

- Split long text with tiktoken or nltk.sent_tokenize and process in batches.
- Keep a cumulative token counter to avoid hitting the 16 k/128 k limits.
- Chunk-then-merge: summarize each chunk, then merge summaries.

Performance Tips

Problem	Fix
Cold start latency	Warm-up the pipeline in server.js before first request
Repeated analysis of same text	Cache embeddings in SQLite or Redis
High memory	Use smaller models (distilbert, albert), or offload to hosted APIs

When to Use Which Provider

Task	Best bet
Sentiment, small-scale	Hugging Face pipeline (local)
Cross-language search	OpenAI embeddings + GPT rerank
Topic modeling	Cohere embed-english-v3.0 + K-Means
Speech-to-text	OpenAI Whisper endpoint

By weaving these NLP steps into your Replit backend you can add moderation, smart search, multilingual chat, and analytics with just a few dozen lines of code—turning static pages into intelligent assistants.

Adding Image Recognition

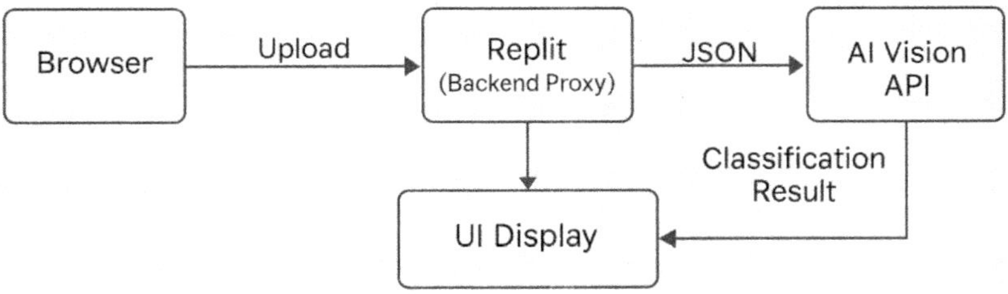

Adding image recognition lets your site understand what a user uploads - whether that's classifying pets, extracting text from receipts, or moderating profile pictures - without running heavy models locally.

How the pieces fit together

The diagram shows the round-trip: browser → Replit proxy → cloud vision API → JSON back to the UI.

1. **Browser** - user selects or snaps a photo.
2. **Upload** - file sent as multipart/form-data to /api/analyze.
3. **Replit backend** - forwards a base64-encoded image to an AI vision API.
4. **AI Vision API** - returns labels, bounding boxes, text, or NSFW flags.

5. **UI Display** - overlays results or shows the best guess.

Choosing a vision provider

Provider	Strengths	Typical endpoint
OpenAI GPT-4o Vision	Multi-modal chat + OCR in one call	/v1/chat/completions (images array)
Google Vision	Rich label / landmark DB	images:annotate
AWS Rekognition	Face detection, celebrity match	DetectFaces, DetectLabels
Hugging Face Spaces	Thousands of open-source models	any run/predict route

Backend proxy (Node + Express)

```
import express from "express";

import multer from "multer";

import fetch from "node-fetch";

import fs from "fs/promises";


const upload = multer({ limits: { fileSize: 4 * 1024 * 1024 } }); // 4
MB

const app = express();
```

```
app.post("/api/analyze", upload.single("image"), async (req, res) =>
{
  // turn buffer → base64
  const b64 = req.file.buffer.toString("base64");
  const payload = {
    model: "gpt-4o-vision-preview",
    messages: [
      {
        role: "user",
        content: [
          { type: "text",  text: "What's in this image?" },
          { type: "image_url", image_url: { b64_json: b64 } }
        ]
      }
    ]
  };

  const upstream = await
fetch("https://api.openai.com/v1/chat/completions", {
    method: "POST",
    headers: {
      "Authorization": `Bearer ${process.env.OPENAI_API_KEY}`,
      "Content-Type": "application/json"
```

```
    },
    body: JSON.stringify(payload)
  });

  if (!upstream.ok) {
    return res.status(502).json({ error: await upstream.text() });
  }
  const data = await upstream.json();
  res.json({ answer: data.choices[0].message.content });
});

app.listen(3000);
```

Why base64? Most hosted APIs accept inline base64 when the image is < 2–4 MB, saving you a temporary object-store upload.

Front-end snippet (React)

```
async function handleFile(e) {
  const file = e.target.files[0];
  const form = new FormData();
  form.append("image", file);

  setStatus("Analyzing…");
  const res = await fetch("/api/analyze", { method: "POST", body: form });
```

```
  const json = await res.json();
  setAnswer(json.answer);
}
```

Best-practice checklist

Concern	Mitigation
Large photos	sharp or pillow to resize → 1024 px
PII in images	Blur faces or redact text with moderation APIs
Latency spikes	Cache common results with MD5(image)
Quota limits	Debounce uploads, 1 req / 5 s per user
Security	Accept only image/*, limit 4 MB

Extending functionality

- **OCR receipts** → pipe recognized text to GPT for expense parsing.
- **Object detection** → draw bounding boxes on <canvas> layer.
- **Similarity search** → embed image with CLIP, match against your gallery in Pinecone.
- **Accessibility alt-text** → generate short descriptions for user-generated images.

With these pieces in place you can drop image understanding into any Replit project - no GPU required, just a few API calls and thoughtful safeguards.

Using Generative AI for Content Creation

The same models that power chatbots can turbo-charge your blog, docs, newsletters, or product descriptions.

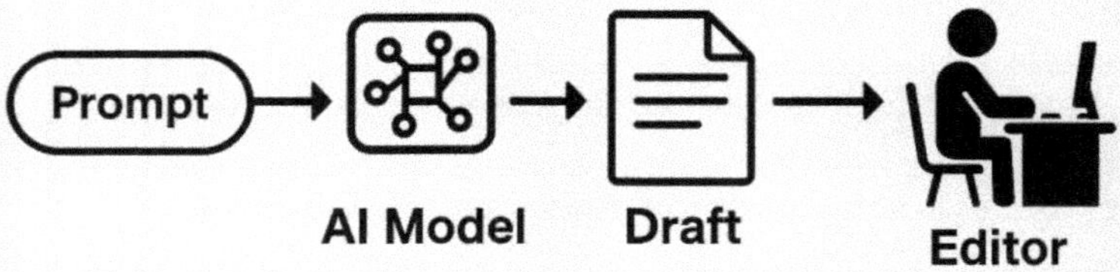

The figure above shows the high-level flow: a prompt goes to an AI model, which returns a draft that you - or an automated post-processor - polish before publishing.

1. Content Types You Can Generate

Medium	Typical Model / Endpoint	Example Use-Case
Blog posts	OpenAI gpt-4o, Anthropic Claude	Long-form articles, how-to guides
Social snippets	Cohere Command-R	Tweets, LinkedIn intros

Medium	Typical Model / Endpoint	Example Use-Case
Marketing copy	Jasper API (OpenAI under the hood)	A/B headlines, landing-page text
Images	OpenAI DALL·E 3, SDXL via Replicate	Hero banners, product visuals
Code	OpenAI gpt-4o-code	Template generators, boilerplate

2. Prompt Engineering Patterns

1. **Role → Task → Context → Format**

"You are a technical copywriter. Write a 250-word feature overview for a JavaScript library. Return in Markdown."

2. **Few-shot**
   Provide 1-2 examples of the style or tone you want, then add ### separator before the new request.

3. **Chain-of-thought** (CoT)
   Ask the model to think step-by-step and then provide the final answer after ---.

Save reusable prompts as constants so you can tweak them without hunting across files.

3. Server-Side Draft Endpoint (Node)

```
import express from "express";

import fetch from "node-fetch";

const app = express();
```

```
app.use(express.json());

app.post("/api/draft", async (req, res) => {
  const { topic, wordCount } = req.body;
  const payload = {
    model: "gpt-4o-mini",
    messages: [{
      role: "user",
      content: `You are a blog author. Write ~${wordCount} words
about "${topic}". Return Markdown.`
    }],
    temperature: 0.7
  };

  const r = await
fetch("https://api.openai.com/v1/chat/completions", {
    method: "POST",
    headers: {
      "Authorization": `Bearer ${process.env.OPENAI_API_KEY}`,
      "Content-Type": "application/json"
    },
    body: JSON.stringify(payload)
  });
```

```
  const json = await r.json();
  res.json({ markdown: json.choices[0].message.content });
});

app.listen(3000);
```

Your CMS can now hit /api/draft to pre-fill the editor.

4. Post-Processing & Guardrails

Check	How to Implement
Length / word count	markdown.split(/\s+/).length
Brand tone	Moderate with a style-guide prompt or Grammarly API
Fact verification	Run generated claims through a search-and-cite pipeline
Plagiarism	Call Copyscape or GPT-4o "does this text exist online?"
Sensitive content	Use OpenAI's moderation endpoint

Fail fast in the backend if content violates policy: respond 403 with a helpful JSON error.

5. Batch Generation with Streaming

Generating dozens of drafts? Send a single chat request per article but stream tokens back. Append each chunk to a file as it arrives to avoid timeouts and keep the UI responsive.

```
const reader = r.body.getReader();
const encoder = new TextDecoder();
let buf = "";
while (true) {
 const { done, value } = await reader.read();
 if (done) break;
 buf += encoder.decode(value, { stream: true });
 if (buf.includes("\n\n")) {
  processChunk(buf);
  buf = "";
 }
}
```

6. Image Creation Pipeline

```
import openai, base64, requests, os
openai.api_key = os.getenv("OPENAI_API_KEY")

def hero_image(prompt):
   resp = openai.images.generate(
      model="dall-e-3", prompt=prompt, n=1, size="1024x1024"
   )
   url = resp.data[0].url
   img = requests.get(url).content
```

```
    return base64.b64encode(img).decode()
```

Embed the returned base64 in an <img> tag to avoid separate storage if the asset is small.

7. Cost Control Tips

- Use smaller models (gpt-3.5-turbo) for outlines, then upscale final copy with GPT-4o.
- Cache identical prompts + parameters by hashing JSON payloads.
- For images, keep n=1 and size 512×512, upscale client-side with JS (window.createImageBitmap) if needed.

8. Human-in-the-Loop Workflow

1. **Draft** → auto-generated via /api/draft.
2. **Edit** → human reviewer tweaks, adds links, fixes style.
3. **Approve** → click publish; script pushes to a Git-backed CMS.
4. **A/B Test** → optional multivariate titles; winning variant picked by analytics.

Track every AI-generated field in your database with created_by_ai: true so legal or marketing can filter & audit later.

By combining structured prompts, guarded pipelines, and human review, you can ship polished content in a fraction of the time without sacrificing brand voice or factual accuracy.

Building Recommendation Systems

A recommendation engine turns user clicks, reads, or listens into personalized suggestions - boosting engagement and time-on-site. Modern AI makes this surprisingly approachable even in a lightweight Replit project.

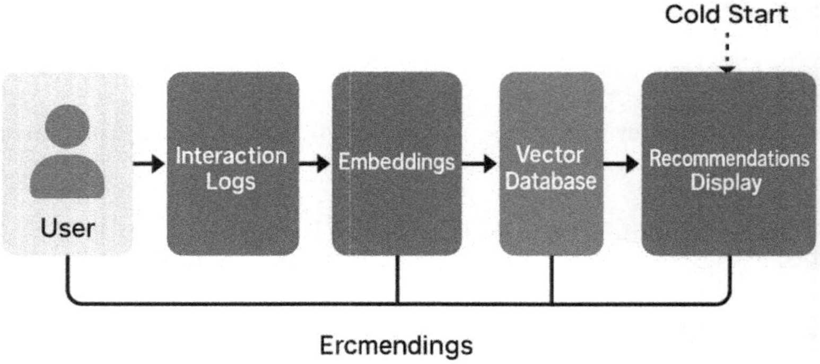

The figure above walks through a common pipeline: user actions → interaction logs → embeddings → vector search → ranked recommendations. The dashed arrow highlights the "cold-start" problem for brand-new users.

1. Recommendation Strategies at a Glance

Approach	Data Needed	Strengths	Weaknesses / Mitigations
Content-based	Item metadata, text, tags	No user history required	Narrow variety → add exploration rate
Collaborative filter	User-item interaction matrix	Captures crowd wisdom	Cold-start → seed with content model

Approach	Data Needed	Strengths	Weaknesses / Mitigations
Embedding similarity	Text or image embeddings	Handles unstructured content	Requires vector DB
Hybrid (recommended)	Combine CB + CF + vectors	Balances novelty & accuracy	Slightly more plumbing

2. Capturing Signals in Replit

```
// log.js – tiny logging helper
export async function logView(userId, itemId) {
  await fetch("/api/log", {
    method: "POST",
    headers: {"Content-Type": "application/json"},
    body: JSON.stringify({ userId, itemId, ts: Date.now() })
  });
}
```

Store these logs in SQLite or Supabase (views(user_id, item_id, ts)).

3. Generating Embeddings with OpenAI

```
import openai, sqlite3, json, os
openai.api_key = os.getenv("OPENAI_API_KEY")
```

```
db = sqlite3.connect("items.db")

db.execute("CREATE TABLE IF NOT EXISTS items(id TEXT, title, vec BLOB)")


def add_item(item_id, title):
    vec = openai.embeddings.create(
        model="text-embedding-3-small",
        input=title
    ).data[0].embedding
    db.execute("INSERT INTO items VALUES(?,?,?)",
               (item_id, title, json.dumps(vec)))
    db.commit()
```

Run once on catalog import or when a new article/product is published.

4. Fast Similarity Search with a Vector DB

Install **LanceDB** (pure Python, no server) or call out to **Pinecone** for production scale.

```
import lancedb, numpy as np, json, sqlite3


ldb = lancedb.connect("vec.lance")

tbl = ldb.create_table("items", schema={"id":"str", "vec":"vector<float>"})


# migrate vectors from SQLite
```

```
for row in db.execute("SELECT id, vec FROM items"):
    tbl.add({"id": row[0], "vec": json.loads(row[1])})


def top_k(query, k=5):
    q_vec = openai.embeddings.create(
        model="text-embedding-3-small", input=query
    ).data[0].embedding
    return tbl.search(q_vec).limit(k).to_list()
```

5. Ranking with Collaborative Signals

```
def rank(user_id, candidates):
    # simple score = sim + log(view_count)
    counts = dict(db.execute(
        "SELECT item_id, COUNT(*) FROM views "
        "WHERE user_id=? GROUP BY item_id", (user_id,)
    ))
    scored = [
        (item, sim + 0.1 * np.log1p(counts.get(item["id"], 0)))
        for item, sim in candidates
    ]
    return sorted(scored, key=lambda x: -x[1])
```

Blend 80 % similarity, 20 % popularity for serendipity.

6. Serving Recommendations (Express)

```
app.get("/api/recs/:userId", async (req, res) => {
  const { userId } = req.params;
  const last = await db.all(
    "SELECT title FROM items ORDER BY RANDOM() LIMIT 1"
  );                    // fall-back query
  const best = await rank(userId, last);
  res.json(best.map(r => r[0])); // return list of items
});
```

Hit this endpoint from your React component; cache results for 5 min in the frontend.

7. Handling the Cold-Start Problem

Scenario	Tactic
New user	Display trending items + category picker
New item	Rely on content embeddings for initial similarity
Sparse logs	Give 10 % of slots to random explore candidates

Track an explore vs. exploit ratio; move it toward exploit as confidence grows.

8. Real-Time Updates with Workers

Replit's scheduled tasks (Cron tab) can rebuild nearest-neighbor indices nightly, or trigger on catalog inserts:

```
replit cron add "0 3 * * *" "python refresh_lancedb.py"
```

9. Metrics to Watch

- **CTR** (click-through rate) of recommended vs. baseline items
- **Dwell time** after clicking a rec
- **Coverage** – what % of catalog ever appears in recs
- **Latency** – keep /api/recs < 150 ms for perceived snappiness

Log these to Supabase or PostHog.

10. Key Takeaways

- Combine textual embeddings with interaction logs for robust recommendations.
- A lightweight vector DB + tiny SQL tables run fine on Replit.
- Cold-start is inevitable—design UI that asks preferences early.
- Measure, A/B test, and iterate; even small tweaks to ranking can lift CTR double-digits.

Armed with this hybrid approach, you can power "You may also like" sections, playlist builders, or personalized dashboards without managing complex ML infra - just smart API calls and a bit of math.

Chapter 7: Enhancing User Interaction

Creating Dynamic and Interactive Elements

AI is only as impressive as the interface that delivers it. Your users won't care about embeddings or token streams unless they're wrapped in a smooth, intuitive experience.

1. Why Interactivity Matters

Modern users expect more than static responses. They expect:

- **Real-time feedback** ("typing…" indicators, loading animations)
- **Editable content** (click-to-edit replies, toggle settings)
- **Visual clarity** (auto-scrolling chat windows, toast notifications)
- **Input affordances** (character counters, disabled buttons, autosize fields)

These features keep users engaged and informed—especially important when responses take several seconds.

2. Typing Indicator with React

JSX

```
{loading && (
  <div className="typing-indicator">
    <span className="dot" />
    <span className="dot" />
    <span className="dot" />
  </div>
```

```
)}
```

CSS

```
.typing-indicator {
  display: flex;
  gap: 0.2rem;
  padding: 0.5rem;
}
.dot {
  width: 6px;
  height: 6px;
  border-radius: 50%;
  background: #999;
  animation: blink 1s infinite alternate;
}
@keyframes blink {
  0%   { opacity: 0.2; }
  100% { opacity: 1; }
}
```

Add this under your AI response bubble while the server is generating a reply.

3. Auto-Scroll Chat History

```
useEffect(() => {
  const el = chatRef.current;
```

```
  if (el) el.scrollTop = el.scrollHeight;
}, [messages]);
```

Keep conversations pinned to the bottom so users always see the latest message without manual scrolling.

4. Autosizing Input Field

```
<textarea
  value={input}
  onChange={e => setInput(e.target.value)}
  rows={1}
  onInput={e => {
    e.target.style.height = "auto";
    e.target.style.height = e.target.scrollHeight + "px";
  }}
/>
```

Prevent jumpy layouts by expanding the text area to fit user input naturally.

5. Toast Notifications

JSX

```
function Toast({ message }) {
  return (
    <div className="toast">{message}</div>
  );
}
```

CSS

```css
.toast {
  position: fixed;
  bottom: 1rem;
  right: 1rem;
  background: #333;
  color: #fff;
  padding: 0.75rem 1rem;
  border-radius: 8px;
  animation: fadein 0.5s ease, fadeout 0.5s ease 2.5s;
}
@keyframes fadein { from { opacity: 0; } to { opacity: 1; } }
@keyframes fadeout { from { opacity: 1; } to { opacity: 0; } }
```

Trigger on errors, saved states, or server responses that don't immediately show on screen.

6. Dynamic Prompts or Personalization

Include recent user context or settings in the prompt dynamically:

```javascript
const payload = {
  messages: [
    { role: "system", content: `You are a helpful assistant for
${user.name}.` },
    ...conversation
  ]
```

```
};
```

Swap in tone, topic, or preferences—without reloading the whole page.

7. Theme Switching (Dark/Light)

Add a toggle to switch CSS variables dynamically:

JS

```
function toggleTheme() {
  document.documentElement.classList.toggle("dark");
}
```

CSS

```
:root {
  --bg: #fff;
  --text: #000;
}
.dark {
  --bg: #111;
  --text: #eee;
}
body {
  background: var(--bg);
  color: var(--text);
}
```

Use prefers-color-scheme media query for automatic initial mode.

8. Real-Time Word Streaming

As tokens arrive from the AI, update state without waiting for the whole reply:

```
const reader = res.body.getReader();
const decoder = new TextDecoder("utf-8");
let buffer = "";

while (true) {
  const { done, value } = await reader.read();
  if (done) break;
  buffer += decoder.decode(value, { stream: true });
  setAI(prev => prev + buffer);
  buffer = "";
}
```

Make the experience feel as fast as autocomplete rather than waiting on a full paragraph.

9. Drag-and-Drop Uploads

```
<div
  onDrop={e => {
    e.preventDefault();
    const file = e.dataTransfer.files[0];
    handleUpload(file);
```

```
  }}
  onDragOver={e => e.preventDefault()}
>
  Drop image here
</div>
```

Accept image/audio files for vision or speech endpoints - add a preview while the upload completes.

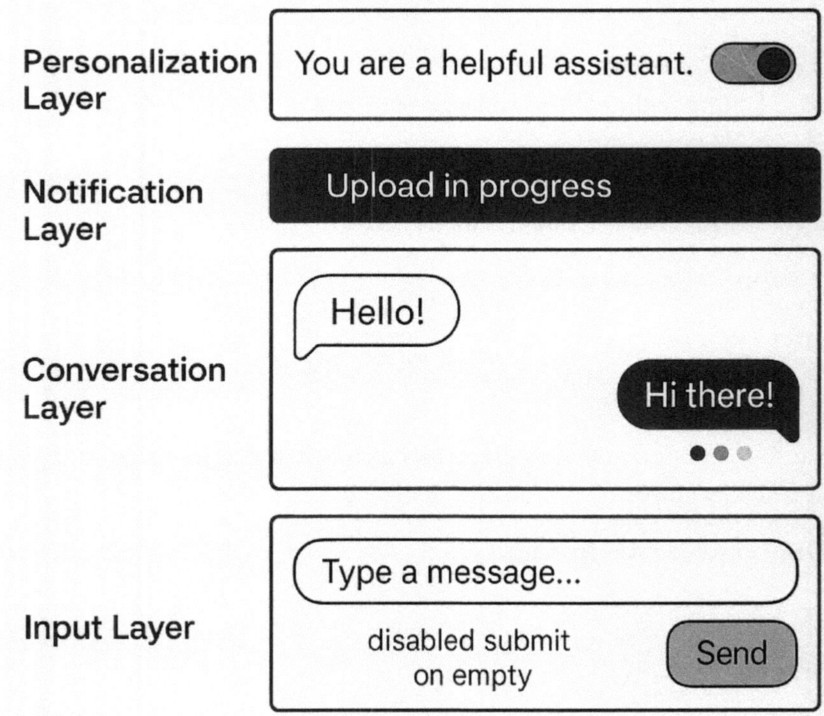

Dynamic UI Layers in AI Apps

10. Diagram: Dynamic UI Layers in AI Apps

The image below maps interactive features to each part of the page:

- **Input Layer**: autosize field, disabled submit on empty
- **Conversation Layer**: bubbles, streaming, loading spinner
- **Notification Layer**: toast alerts, upload progress
- **Personalization Layer**: theme toggle, settings-based prompts

(See visual in the figure above)

By thoughtfully layering interactive elements - from subtle animations to contextual awareness - you transform an API-driven chatbot into a modern, friendly assistant. The effort pays off in user trust, lower bounce rates, and better retention.

Managing User Input and AI Responses

Handling input and output isn't just about sending a prompt and printing a reply. A robust pipeline - like the one in *the figure below* - protects your app from abuse, keeps latency predictable, and ensures every response arrives in the right format.

1. Sanitizing & Validating Input

Check	Why	How to implement
Empty / whitespace	Avoid needless calls	Disable **Send** button if draft.trim().length === 0
Length limit	Prevent 128 k-token bombs	if (tokens > 4 000) return 413
HTML/JS injection	XSS defense for display	DOMPurify or server-side strip tags

Check	Why	How to implement
Rate limit	Throttle spam	express-rate-limit → 10 req / min / IP

2. Token Counting Before You Send

```
import { encoding_for_model } from "@dqbd/tiktoken";


const enc = encoding_for_model("gpt-4o-mini");
const tokens = enc.encode(userText).length;
if (tokens > 4000) throw new Error("Prompt too long!");
```

Early failure > expensive rejection from the provider.

3. Queue & Concurrency Control

```
import PQueue from "p-queue";
const queue = new PQueue({ concurrency: 3 }); // 3 simultaneous calls


router.post("/api/chat", async (req, res) => {
  await queue.add(() => handleChat(req, res));
});
```

Keeps your Replit container from spawning 50 parallel fetches under load.

4. Streaming & Partial Updates

1. **Open a reader** on the response body.

2. **Append tokens** to the last AI bubble as they arrive (see earlier code).
3. **Handle disconnects**—if the user navigates away, abort the fetch with AbortController.

5. Post-Processing Responses

Task	Example
Markdown → HTML	marked.parse(response)
Code block syntax highlighting	highlight.js
Linkify URLs	linkify-html
Moderation	Check with OpenAI /moderations before display

Skip heavy transforms (like large regex) inside the streaming loop; apply them after the stream finishes.

6. Error Surfacing to the UI

```
try {
  await send();
} catch (e) {
  toast(`⚠️ ${e.message}`);
}
```

Return structured JSON errors from the server:

```
{ "error": "rate_limit", "retry_in": 30 }
```

Your client can disable the input and show a countdown instead of a generic "Something went wrong."

7. Caching Frequent Requests

For deterministic utilities (e.g., summarize URL), hash the prompt + parameters and store the full AI reply in SQLite/Redis for 24 h. Respond immediately when the same query returns.

8. Logging for Debugging

Store anonymized fields:

Field	Purpose
hash(userId)	Tie requests to sessions
prompt_size	Spot outliers
latency_ms	Track provider slowness
error_code	Alert on spikes

Send to Logtail or Replit's Logs for quick triage.

9. End-to-End Flow (see diagram)

1. **User Message**
2. **Sanitizer** – strip HTML, trim, check length
3. **Token Count** – detect over-limit prompts
4. **Queue / Rate Limit** – back-pressure heavy traffic
5. **AI** – call provider, stream response
6. **Post-Processor** – Markdown → HTML, moderation

7. **Display** – render bubbles, auto-scroll, toast on error

Each stage is a guardrail - fail fast, inform the user, keep the app healthy.

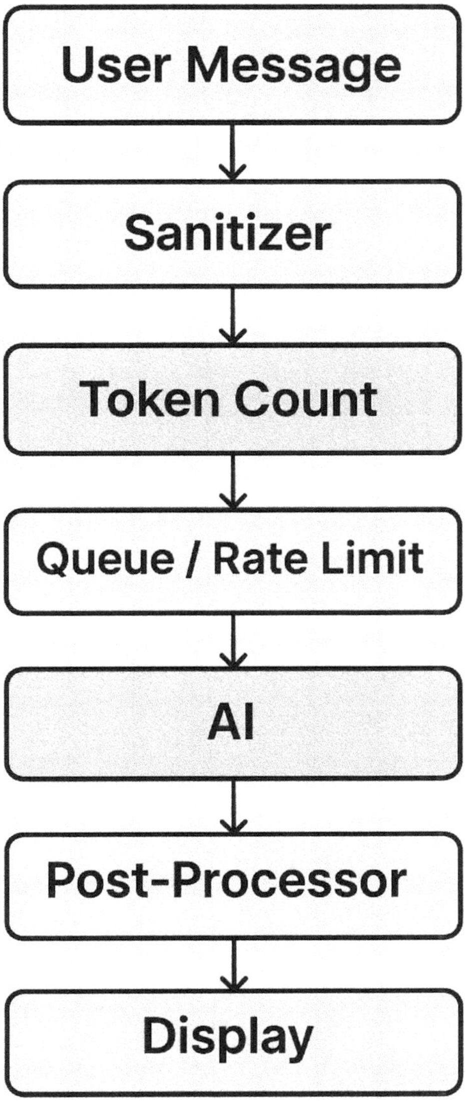

Key Takeaways

- Validate early, fail fast, and inform users clearly.
- Stream for perceived speed but post-process for polish.
- Throttle requests server-side to survive traffic spikes.
- Log enough context to debug without storing raw PII.

Master these patterns and every new AI feature you add will inherit rock-solid UX from day one.

Adding Real-Time Features

Real-time features make AI web apps feel responsive, connected, and alive. Whether you're streaming messages as they generate, showing typing indicators, or pushing live updates to multiple users, these capabilities elevate user trust and experience.

Why Real-Time Matters

Static interfaces feel disconnected. In contrast, real-time feedback:

- **Builds trust**: Showing that the model is "thinking" reassures users during latency.
- **Improves usability**: Streaming responses lets users read answers as they appear.
- **Enables collaboration**: Users can see each other's changes in multiplayer apps.
- **Feels alive**: Notifications, updates, and system feedback feel instant and modern.

Real-Time Use Cases in AI-Powered Web Apps

Feature	Tool/Protocol	Description
Streaming AI responses	SSE / Fetch	Display output tokens as they arrive
Typing indicators	WebSocket / Polling	Show when the AI or user is generating content
Live chat / co-editing	WebSocket	Real-time collaboration and updates
Push notifications	SSE / WebSocket	Alert users to background AI activity
File upload progress	XMLHttpRequest	Show visual progress for image/audio processing

Streaming AI Responses with Server-Sent Events (SSE)

SSE is a perfect match for AI outputs that generate text incrementally. Replit's always-on Node server works well with it.

Backend Example (Node + Express):

```
app.post("/api/chat", async (req, res) => {
  res.setHeader("Content-Type", "text/event-stream");
  res.setHeader("Cache-Control", "no-cache");
  res.setHeader("Connection", "keep-alive");
  const upstream = await
fetch("https://api.openai.com/v1/chat/completions", {
    method: "POST",
```

```
    headers: {
      "Authorization": `Bearer ${process.env.OPENAI_API_KEY}`,
      "Content-Type": "application/json"
    },
    body: JSON.stringify({
      model: "gpt-4o",
      stream: true,
      messages: req.body.messages
    })
  });

  for await (const chunk of upstream.body) {
    res.write(`data: ${chunk.toString()}\n\n`);
  }

  res.write("data: [DONE]\n\n");
  res.end();
});
```

Frontend Example (React):

```
function streamReply(messages, onToken) {
  const evtSource = new EventSource("/api/chat");
  let buffer = "";
```

```
  evtSource.onmessage = (event) => {
    if (event.data === "[DONE]") return evtSource.close();
    buffer += event.data;
    onToken(buffer); // partial render
    buffer = "";
  };

  evtSource.onerror = (err) => {
    console.error("Stream failed", err);
    evtSource.close();
  };
}
```

Update the last chat bubble in state with each new token for a live-typing effect.

Real-Time Typing Indicator with WebSocket

For real-time multiplayer or chatbot typing signals, WebSockets let you push and receive low-latency messages bi-directionally.

```
// Client
const socket = new WebSocket("wss://yourapp.replit.app/ws");
function sendTyping(isTyping) {
  socket.send(JSON.stringify({ type: "typing", status: isTyping }));
}
```

```
socket.onmessage = (e) => {
  const data = JSON.parse(e.data);
  if (data.type === "typing") showIndicator(data.status);
};
```

Use Replit's WebSocket-compatible server libraries like ws for small rooms or collaborative features.

Showing Upload Progress in Real Time

For AI that analyzes images/audio, show live upload status:

```
const xhr = new XMLHttpRequest();
xhr.open("POST", "/api/upload");
xhr.upload.onprogress = (e) => {
  const percent = Math.round((e.loaded / e.total) * 100);
  setProgress(percent);
};
xhr.send(formData);
```

Use <progress> tags or animated bars to reflect upload state visually.

Building Notifications with SSE

Push alerts like "Your analysis is ready" without polling:

```
// backend
app.get("/api/events", (req, res) => {
  res.setHeader("Content-Type", "text/event-stream");
  res.write("data: { \"event\": \"connected\" }\n\n");
```

```
 setTimeout(() => {
   res.write("data: { \"event\": \"ready\", \"msg\": \"Your summary is done.\" }\n\n");
 }, 5000);
});

// frontend
const evt = new EventSource("/api/events");
evt.onmessage = e => {
 const { event, msg } = JSON.parse(e.data);
 if (event === "ready") toast(msg);
};
```

Diagram: Real-Time Layers in an AI App

See the figure below - Real-Time UX Layers
The diagram shows a layered view from user actions (input, upload) through backend events (streaming, state changes), and back to the UI.

- **Input Layer** → keypress events, form changes
- **Transport Layer** → Fetch (SSE), WebSocket
- **Response Layer** → token updates, AI responses, notifications
- **Feedback Layer** → spinners, typing indicators, progress bars

This architecture ensures the app feels reactive, even when responses take 5+ seconds.

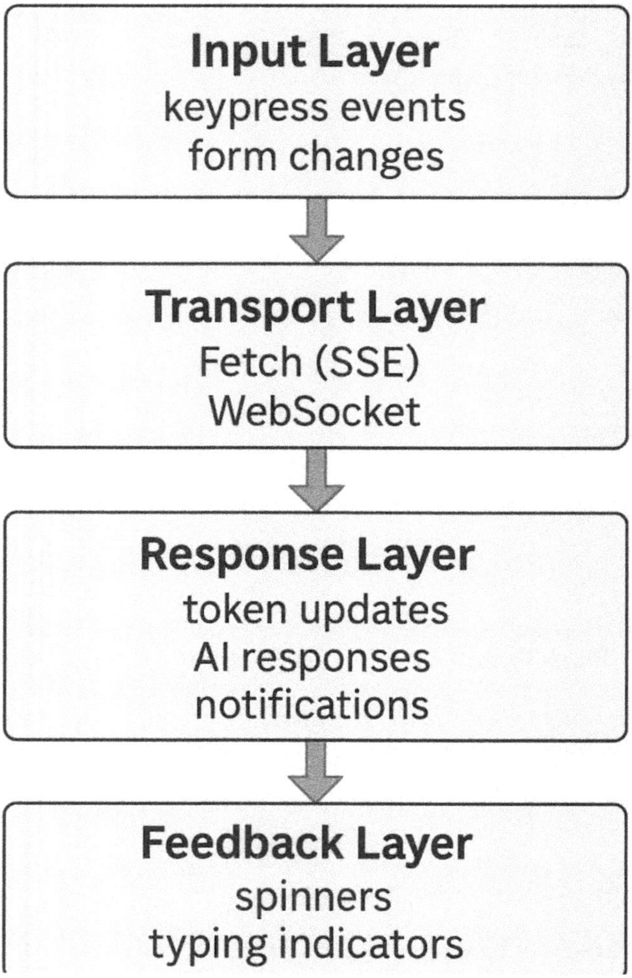

Final Tips for Real-Time UX

- **Debounce keystrokes** to reduce over-communication (300 ms)
- **Gracefully disconnect** streams on tab close (AbortController)

- **Fallback** to full-response if streaming fails
- **Test latency** across network conditions with Chrome DevTools

Real-time features are essential for keeping users engaged and reducing perceived wait times in AI web apps. With tools like Server-Sent Events, WebSockets, and browser-native APIs, you can build fast, modern, and reactive experiences in Replit without deploying external infrastructure.

Improving UX and Accessibility

Designing intelligent web applications isn't just about functionality. The experience - the way users *feel* using your app - matters just as much. A well-built AI-powered site should feel fast, intuitive, inclusive, and responsive, even under load.

Why UX and Accessibility Matter in AI Apps

AI interfaces often deal with:

- **Unpredictable latency** (e.g. model streaming),
- **Complex outputs** (e.g. Markdown, charts),
- **Diverse users** (screen readers, keyboard-only navigation).

Poor UX and accessibility can turn smart functionality into frustrating friction.

Good design ensures:

✅ Everyone can use it
✅ Responses arrive clearly
✅ Errors are obvious, recoverable
✅ The interface feels trustworthy and intuitive

1. Clear Input-AI-Output Flow

Visual structure helps users understand where they are in a task.

Layer	UX Pattern
Input	Labelled fields, autosize textarea, voice input optional
Processing	Loading spinners, token streamers, "Thinking…" badges
Output	AI bubble, copy-to-clipboard, Markdown rendering
Feedback/Error	Inline error messages, retry buttons, toast notifications

Use card layouts and whitespace to separate inputs and responses.

2. Responsive Design Across Devices

Ensure your site looks good on phones, tablets, and desktops.

```
@media (max-width: 768px) {
  .chat-window {
    font-size: 0.95rem;
    padding: 0.5rem;
  }
  .sidebar { display: none; }
}
```

Use flex or grid to allow dynamic resizing and wrapping:

```
.chat-area {
```

```
  display: flex;
  flex-direction: column;
  max-height: 80vh;
  overflow-y: auto;
}
```

3. Keyboard-Only Navigation

Enable seamless tabbing and activation:

```
<button
  onClick={send}
  onKeyDown={(e) => { if (e.key === "Enter") send(); }}
  tabIndex="0"
>
  Send
</button>
```

Use visible focus rings:

```
:focus {
  outline: 2px solid #00f;
}
```

4. Screen Reader Support

Use semantic HTML and aria-* attributes:

```
<label htmlFor="message">Your message</label>
<textarea id="message" aria-label="Chat input" />
```

For AI responses, consider role="log" to let screen readers pick up dynamic updates:

```
<div role="log" aria-live="polite">
  {messages.map((msg, i) => (
   <p key={i}>{msg.content}</p>
 ))}
</div>
```

5. Loading and AI Status Indicators

Instead of freezing the UI, communicate clearly:

```
{loading && <span aria-live="assertive">Bot is typing…</span>}
```

Add spinners with screen-reader-friendly labels:

```
<div class="spinner" role="status" aria-label="Loading reply" />
```

6. Error Recovery and Help

Users should never feel stuck.

- Provide **retry** buttons on failed requests
- Use **toasts** to surface transient issues (setTimeout(() => hideToast(), 3000))
- Add a **FAQ or hint button** that toggles a help panel

```
{error && (
  <div className="error">
   Something went wrong. <button onClick={retry}>Try again</button>
  </div>
```

```
)}
```

7. Visual Feedback for Long Tasks

If AI is generating a summary, show a progress bar or message that adjusts over time.

```
setTimeout(() => setMsg("Still working... almost there!"), 4000);
```

Avoid "invisible waits"—they frustrate and confuse users.

8. Accessible Color Palettes and Contrast

Maintain **minimum contrast** ratios:

- Text vs background: 4.5:1 for body, 3:1 for large headings

Use tools like WebAIM Contrast Checker or install browser extensions to test this visually.

Example theme variables:

```
:root {
  --text-main: #111;
  --bg-light: #fff;
  --accent: #005fcc;
}
```

9. Diagram: UX & a11y Layers in an AI Web App

See the figure below shows a multi-layer diagram showing:

- **Input Layer**: labelled fields, keyboard nav
- **Processing Layer**: loading state, retry UI
- **Output Layer**: readable, screen-reader-friendly AI response
- **Support Layer**: Help button, theme toggle, toasts

This stack ensures a full journey - from form to feedback - is smooth and inclusive.

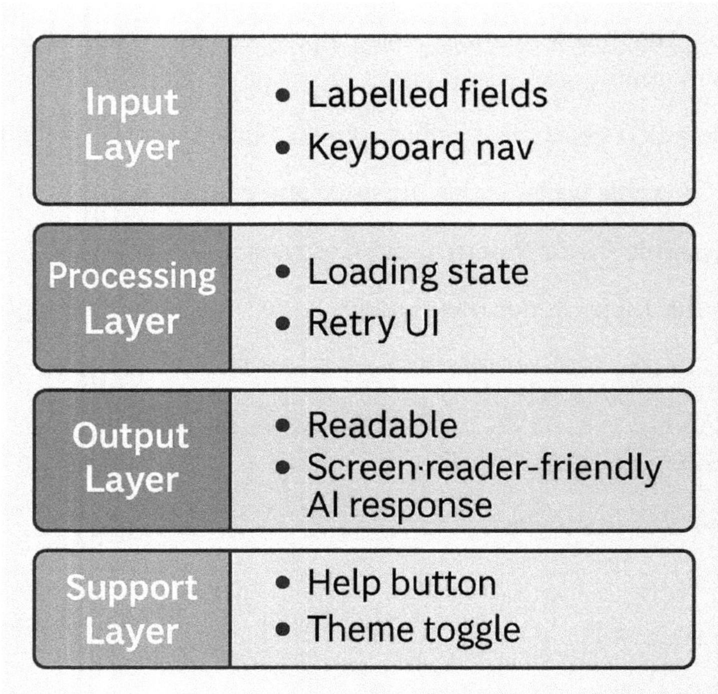

10. Final Checklist

Before you ship your AI site, verify:

- ✅ Tab key works across the interface
- ✅ All buttons and inputs have aria-labels
- ✅ UI responds at every latency point
- ✅ Contrast passes WCAG 2.1 AA
- ✅ Errors are recoverable, not fatal
- ✅ You've tested on desktop + mobile

Improving UX and accessibility transforms your AI web app from a clever demo into a usable, inclusive product. On Replit, with just a few semantic tags, responsive layouts, and feedback loops, you can build experiences that everyone can enjoy - regardless of ability, device, or tech comfort level.

Chapter 8: Database Integration

Choosing and Setting Up Databases in Replit

AI apps quickly outgrow "just-in-memory" storage. You need persistence - whether it's user accounts, chat logs, embeddings, or analytics. Replit supports several paths, each with trade-offs. *See the below figure* that offers a quick decision tree.

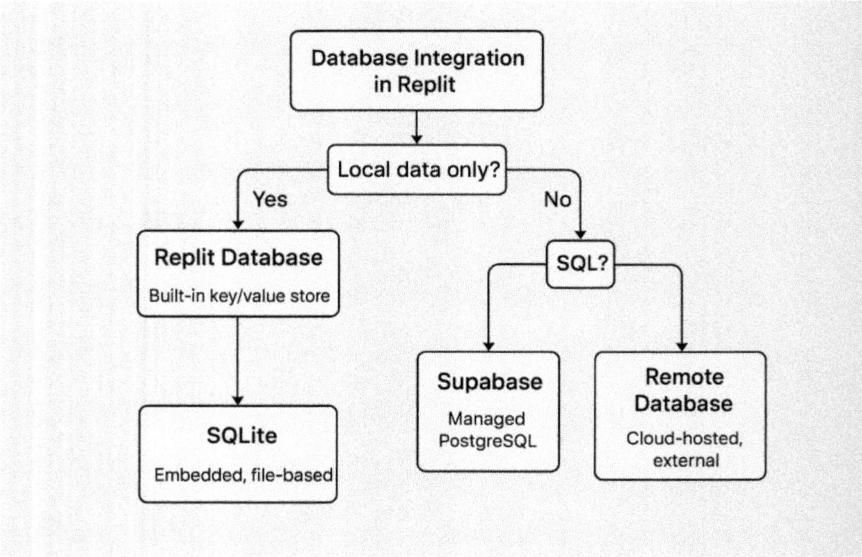

1. Replit Database (Key/Value)

Feature	Details
Type	Simple key/value JSON store
Best for	Prototyping, small user prefs, feature flags
Capacity	50 MB free; pay-as-you-grow
API	import Database from "@replit/database"

Setup

bash

```
npm install @replit/database
```

js

```
import Database from "@replit/database";
const db = new Database();


await db.set("username:42", "dr-mo");
const name = await db.get("username:42");
```

Pros: zero config, no external creds.
Cons: no SQL queries, limited size, latency rises with dataset.

2. SQLite (Embedded SQL)

Feature	Details
Type	File-based relational DB (.sqlite file)
Best for	Local dev, small production apps, vector tables
Capacity	GBs (bounded by Replit storage)
API	better-sqlite3, sqlite3, or Python's sqlite3

Setup (Node)

bash

```
npm install better-sqlite3
```

js

```
import Database from "better-sqlite3";
```

```
const db = new Database("data.sqlite");

db.prepare("CREATE TABLE IF NOT EXISTS msgs(id INTEGER, body TEXT)").run();

db.prepare("INSERT INTO msgs(body) VALUES(?)").run("Hello!");

const rows = db.prepare("SELECT * FROM msgs").all();
```

Add data.sqlite to .gitignore so large files aren't pushed.

3. Supabase (Hosted PostgreSQL)

Supabase gives you a Postgres database, REST & GraphQL API, row-level security, and auth—all free for hobby use.

Feature	Details
Type	Managed PostgreSQL
Best for	Production SaaS, auth + file storage
Capacity	500 MB free tier
API	@supabase/supabase-js client

Setup

1. Create project at **app.supabase.com**.
2. Grab SUPABASE_URL and SUPABASE_KEY, add to Replit Secrets.
3. Install client:

bash

```bash
npm install @supabase/supabase-js
```

js

```js
import { createClient } from "@supabase/supabase-js";
const supabase = createClient(
  process.env.SUPABASE_URL,
  process.env.SUPABASE_KEY
);

const { data, error } = await supabase
  .from("messages")
  .insert({ user_id: 42, body: "Hi!" });
```

Pros: SQL power, row-level policies, built-in auth.
Cons: network latency, separate dashboard to manage.

4. Remote Databases (PlanetScale, Neon, Mongo Atlas)

Need MySQL, Postgres, or MongoDB at scale? Point your Replit app to a cloud DB.

Checklist

- Add connection string (URI) to Secrets.
- Use connection pooling (e.g., pg-pool)—Replit opens/closes frequently.
- Restrict IPs or use SSL certs.

Example (Postgres + pg):

```js
import pkg from "pg";
const { Pool } = pkg;
```

const pool = new Pool({ connectionString: process.env.PG_URI, ssl: true });

const res = await pool.query("SELECT now()");

5. Choosing the Right Store

Need	Recommended
1-day hackathon	Replit DB
Lightweight SQL, local	SQLite
Full-stack app, auth	Supabase
High-volume prod	PlanetScale / Neon / Atlas
Vector search	LanceDB or pgvector on Postgres

6. Migration Tips

- **Start local, go remote**: export SQLite with sqlite3 .dump | psql into Postgres.
- **Secret rotation**: store creds in Secrets tab; rotate monthly.
- **Backups**: Supabase auto-backups; for SQLite, copy the file to /mnt/data nightly.
- **ORMs**: Prisma, Drizzle, or TypeORM work fine—just remember to run prisma generate after installs.

7. Sample Folder Layout

```
repl/
├── server/
│   ├── db.js        # wraps queries
│   ├── routes/
│   └── ...
├── data.sqlite      # git-ignored
├── prisma/
└── .env             # local dev creds
```

Keep DB code in its own module; swap implementations (ReplitDB → Supabase) without touching routes.

With the right database in place, you're ready to persist user state, store embeddings, and collect analytics - unlocking serious AI product capabilities on Replit.

CRUD Operations (Create, Read, Update, Delete)

Once your Replit app is connected to a database - whether Replit DB, SQLite, or Supabase - it's time to start performing real data operations. These operations are often summarized as **CRUD**: Create, Read, Update, and Delete.

Why CRUD Is Core to AI Web Apps

In intelligent web apps, CRUD powers the experience:

Feature	Behind the scenes
Saving chats	**Create** new records in DB

Feature	Behind the scenes
Viewing history	**Read** past messages
Editing user settings	**Update** stored preferences
Deleting saved files	**Delete** specific rows or keys

Well-structured CRUD logic ensures your AI assistant feels persistent, personal, and secure.

1. CREATE – Adding New Data

Let's say a user submits a new message to your chatbot.

Replit DB (Key/Value)

```
await db.set("chat:123", "How do I build a chatbot?");
```

SQLite

```
db.prepare("INSERT INTO messages(user_id, body) VALUES(?, ?)").run(42, "Hello!");
```

Supabase

```
await supabase.from("messages").insert([{ user_id: 42, body: "Hello!" }]);
```

Tip: Always validate input before saving. Watch for SQL injection, even with parameterized queries.

2. READ – Fetching Stored Data

To retrieve chat history or user profiles:

Replit DB

```
const val = await db.get("chat:123");
```

SQLite

```
const rows = db.prepare("SELECT * FROM messages WHERE user_id = ?").all(42);
```

Supabase

```
const { data, error } = await supabase
  .from("messages")
  .select("*")
  .eq("user_id", 42);
```

Use pagination for large datasets: LIMIT 10 OFFSET 20.

3. UPDATE – Changing Data

Maybe the user edited their name or changed a saved note.

Replit DB

```
await db.set("user:42:name", "Dr MO");
```

SQLite

```
db.prepare("UPDATE users SET name = ? WHERE id = ?").run("Dr MO", 42);
```

Supabase

```
await supabase.from("users").update({ name: "Dr MO" }).eq("id", 42);
```

Use PATCH-style updates—only send what changed.

4. DELETE – Removing Data

When users delete a message or clear chat history:

Replit DB

await db.delete("chat:123");

SQLite

```
db.prepare("DELETE FROM messages WHERE id = ?").run(123);
```

Supabase

```
await supabase.from("messages").delete().eq("id", 123);
```

Confirm deletion in the UI before sending the request. If it's sensitive data, consider soft-deletes by adding a deleted_at column instead of removing the row.

5. REST API Layer (Node + Express)

Wrap your CRUD in routes:

```
app.post("/api/messages", async (req, res) => {
  const { user_id, body } = req.body;
  await db.prepare("INSERT INTO messages(user_id, body)
VALUES(?, ?)").run(user_id, body);
  res.status(201).send("Saved");
});


app.get("/api/messages/:uid", async (req, res) => {
  const rows = db.prepare("SELECT * FROM messages WHERE
user_id = ?").all(req.params.uid);
  res.json(rows);
});
```

You can now call these from your frontend with fetch.

6. Frontend Example (React)

```
async function createMessage(body) {
  await fetch("/api/messages", {
    method: "POST",
    headers: { "Content-Type": "application/json" },
    body: JSON.stringify({ user_id: 42, body })
  });
}


async function loadMessages() {
  const res = await fetch("/api/messages/42");
  const json = await res.json();
  setMessages(json);
}
```

Use useEffect() to load data on mount, and update the UI after each create or delete.

7. Diagram: CRUD Operations in Action

The following image (Figure 11-2) shows how each CRUD action maps to a part of your AI app lifecycle:

- **Create** – User sends message → store it
- **Read** – Load old messages on page load
- **Update** – User edits input or settings
- **Delete** – Remove a chat or user account

Each action flows through your frontend → API route → database, then back to the UI.

8. Error Handling Best Practices

Operation	Common Error	Recommended Handling
Create	Invalid data	Return 400 Bad Request with JSON msg
Read	Not found	Return 404 or []
Update	Unauthorized update	Check ownership before updating
Delete	Double delete	Check existence first; return 204

Always log errors server-side for later debugging. Use structured JSON in error responses ({ error: "not_found" }).

Understanding CRUD operations is essential to managing any user-driven data in your Replit app. Whether you're saving chat logs, updating user preferences, or handling deletions, these patterns keep your app consistent and stateful.

By pairing clean CRUD routes with dynamic frontends and proper error handling, you can build intelligent web applications that feel truly interactive, persistent, and robust.

Storing and Retrieving AI-Generated Data

AI-powered apps generate valuable data - chat responses, summaries, tags, labels, embeddings - that can be stored, reused, searched, and analyzed. In Replit, persisting this output means your site can offer features like history, autosuggestions, analytics, and personalized interactions across sessions.

Why Store AI Data?

Data Type	Use Case
AI-generated messages	Chat history, customer support logs
Summaries / paraphrases	Fast previews, document overviews
Tags / classifications	Content filtering, recommendations
Embeddings	Similarity search, clustering, memory
Code completions	Autocomplete, user reference
Moderation decisions	Safety auditing, review queues

Stored AI output lets you avoid redundant API calls, improve performance, and build richer features over time.

1. Storing Chat History

Let's say you're building an AI chatbot. You want to save the conversation in a structured table.

SQLite Schema Example:

```
CREATE TABLE IF NOT EXISTS messages (
  id INTEGER PRIMARY KEY AUTOINCREMENT,
  user_id TEXT,
  role TEXT,         -- 'user' or 'assistant'
  content TEXT,
  ts DATETIME DEFAULT CURRENT_TIMESTAMP
);
```

Insert a message:

```
db.prepare(
  "INSERT INTO messages (user_id, role, content) VALUES (?, ?, ?)"
).run("user123", "assistant", "Here's a summary of your input...");
```

Fetch last 10 messages:

```
const messages = db.prepare(
  "SELECT role, content FROM messages WHERE user_id = ? ORDER BY ts DESC LIMIT 10"
).all("user123");
```

2. Saving Embeddings for Similarity Search

Embeddings (vectors) let you compare meaning between items. Use them to enable search, memory, or clustering.

Storing Embeddings in SQLite:

```
CREATE TABLE IF NOT EXISTS vectors (
  id TEXT PRIMARY KEY,
  text TEXT,
  embedding TEXT  -- store as JSON array
);
```

Insert an embedding:

```
const { data } = await openai.embeddings.create({
  input: "How do I make a chatbot?",
  model: "text-embedding-3-small"
```

```
});

const embedding = JSON.stringify(data[0].embedding);
db.prepare(
  "INSERT INTO vectors (id, text, embedding) VALUES (?, ?, ?)"
).run("msg123", "How do I make a chatbot?", embedding);
```

Retrieve and compare:

Use cosine similarity in JS or load into a vector DB like LanceDB.

3. Caching AI Responses

You can avoid re-processing the same input repeatedly by hashing prompts.

Cache Table:

```
CREATE TABLE IF NOT EXISTS cache (
  hash TEXT PRIMARY KEY,
  prompt TEXT,
  response TEXT,
  ts DATETIME DEFAULT CURRENT_TIMESTAMP
);
```

On every request:

```
const hash =
crypto.createHash("sha1").update(prompt).digest("hex");
```

```
const cached = db.prepare("SELECT response FROM cache WHERE hash = ?").get(hash);


if (cached) {
  return cached.response;
}


const aiRes = await openai.chat.completions.create({ messages });
db.prepare("INSERT INTO cache (hash, prompt, response) VALUES (?, ?, ?)")
  .run(hash, prompt, aiRes.choices[0].message.content);
```

4. Using Supabase for Persistent AI Logs

If you prefer a managed backend with web access and auth:

```
CREATE TABLE messages (
  id UUID PRIMARY KEY,
  user_id UUID,
  role TEXT,
  content TEXT,
  ts TIMESTAMP DEFAULT now()
);
```

Insert from Replit:

```
await supabase
  .from("messages")
```

```
  .insert([{ user_id: "u123", role: "assistant", content: "Here's your summary..." }]);
```

Fetch chat history:

```
const { data } = await supabase
  .from("messages")
  .select("*")
  .eq("user_id", "u123")
  .order("ts", { ascending: false });
```

5. Diagram: Storing AI Data Flow

See the figure below - This diagram maps the round-trip:

1. **User sends input →**
2. **Frontend sends request →**
3. **AI API responds →**
4. **Backend stores result in database**
5. **Frontend renders reply**
6. **History or analytics fetch from DB**

Layers include:

- Input buffer
- API call with prompt
- Database write (messages, vectors)
- Frontend fetch → display

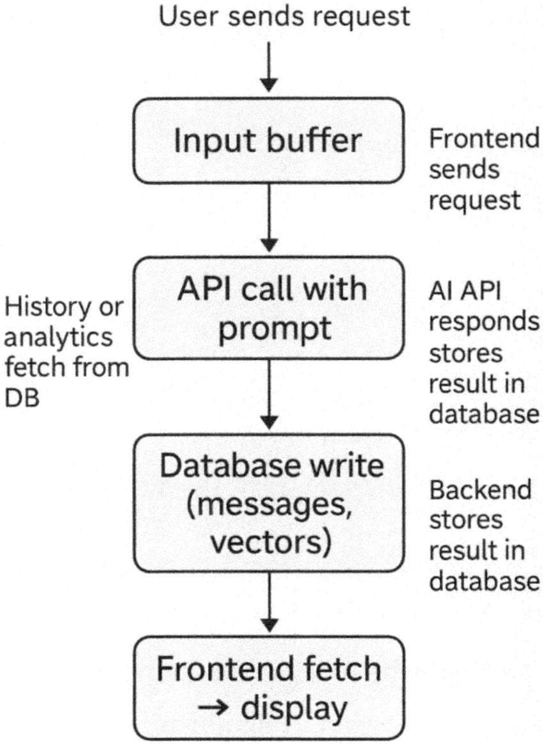

Daragmo shows Storing AI-genrated Data

6. Access Control and Cleanup

- Add a user_id column to everything.
- Use LIMIT + ORDER BY ts DESC to avoid unbounded queries.
- Periodically delete old logs with a background script:

db.prepare("DELETE FROM messages WHERE ts < DATETIME('now', '-30 days')").run();

Or mark messages with archived = 1.

7. AI Data Types and Best Practices

Data Type	Format	Store As	Notes
Text Output	string	TEXT or VARCHAR	No limit unless GPT-4 can exceed
Embeddings	float[]	JSON or vector[]	Use pgvector or encode in JSON
Categories	strings/tags	CSV or join table	Split tag1,tag2 or store separately
Timestamps	ISO 8601	DATETIME	Use CURRENT_TIMESTAMP default
Token usage	number	INTEGER	For billing or analytics

AI-generated data is only as useful as your ability to store and retrieve it efficiently. Whether you're caching completions, building embeddings, or saving full chat histories, Replit gives you tools like SQLite and Supabase to structure and persist that data effectively.

Securing Data and Ensuring Privacy

In any intelligent web application, data is the core asset. Whether your site uses AI to personalize user experiences, recommend products, or process real-time feedback, you are inevitably handling sensitive information.

Why Security and Privacy Matter

With the increasing prevalence of data breaches and misuse of personal data, users are more privacy-conscious than ever. Legal regulations such as the **General Data Protection Regulation**

(GDPR) in the EU, **California Consumer Privacy Act (CCPA)** in the US, and others globally, impose strict requirements on how data must be handled. Beyond legal compliance, good data practices build trust and protect your application's integrity.

Key Concepts in Database Security and Privacy

1. Data Encryption

- **In transit:** Use HTTPS to encrypt data transmitted between the client and the server.
- **At rest:** Encrypt sensitive data in the database. For example, passwords should never be stored in plain text; use hashing algorithms like bcrypt.

2. Authentication and Authorization

- Implement **user authentication** (e.g., email/password, OAuth2) and **role-based access control** (RBAC).
- Use token-based authentication such as **JWT** (JSON Web Tokens) to maintain secure sessions.

3. Minimal Privilege Principle

- Grant only the minimum necessary permissions to users and services. Avoid giving full admin rights unless absolutely required.

4. Environment Variable Management

- Never hardcode credentials in your codebase. Replit allows you to use **Secrets** (environment variables) to securely store API keys, database URIs, and other sensitive information.

5. Input Validation and Sanitization

- Use server-side validation and input sanitization to prevent **SQL injection** and **NoSQL injection** attacks.

- Consider using ORMs like **SQLAlchemy** (for Python) or **Mongoose** (for MongoDB in Node.js) which include built-in protection mechanisms.

6. Secure Backup and Recovery

- Schedule automated encrypted backups of your database and store them securely.
- Ensure you have a recovery plan in place for accidental data loss or corruption.

7. Privacy by Design

- Minimize data collection. Only ask for and store data that is strictly necessary.
- Allow users to view, export, and delete their data in compliance with privacy laws.
- Use **anonymization** or **pseudonymization** when working with large datasets for training AI models.

Practical Implementation Example: Securing a MongoDB Integration on Replit

Step 1: Store Credentials Safely

On Replit, use the **Secrets** tab to store your MongoDB URI:

```
import os

from pymongo import MongoClient


MONGO_URI = os.getenv("MONGO_URI")

client = MongoClient(MONGO_URI)

db = client["user_data"]
```

Step 2: Hash Passwords Before Storage

```
from werkzeug.security import generate_password_hash


password = "user_password"

hashed_password = generate_password_hash(password)

db.users.insert_one({"username": "johndoe", "password":
hashed_password})
```

Step 3: Use HTTPS and JWT for Authentication

Ensure your Replit project uses HTTPS and a JWT library like pyjwt to secure routes that require authentication.

Ensuring Privacy in AI Models

If your intelligent website includes machine learning components:

- Never train AI models on raw personal data. Aggregate or anonymize datasets.
- Be transparent about AI decision-making and allow opt-outs where possible.
- Avoid data over-collection by implementing client-side controls (e.g., toggles, form limits).

[Illustrative Image Description]

Title: "Layers of Data Protection in AI Web Apps"

Visual Structure:
A multi-layered shield graphic with the following concentric layers, each labeled:

1. **User Interface (Outer Layer)** – Input validation, HTTPS
2. **API Layer** – Authentication & token validation

3. **Backend Logic** – Access controls, role validation
4. **Database** – Encrypted data, hashed credentials
5. **Storage & Backup** – Encrypted backup, disaster recovery
6. **AI Model** – Anonymized inputs, transparency protocols

At the side: GDPR, CCPA icons with arrows pointing to legal compliance indicators.

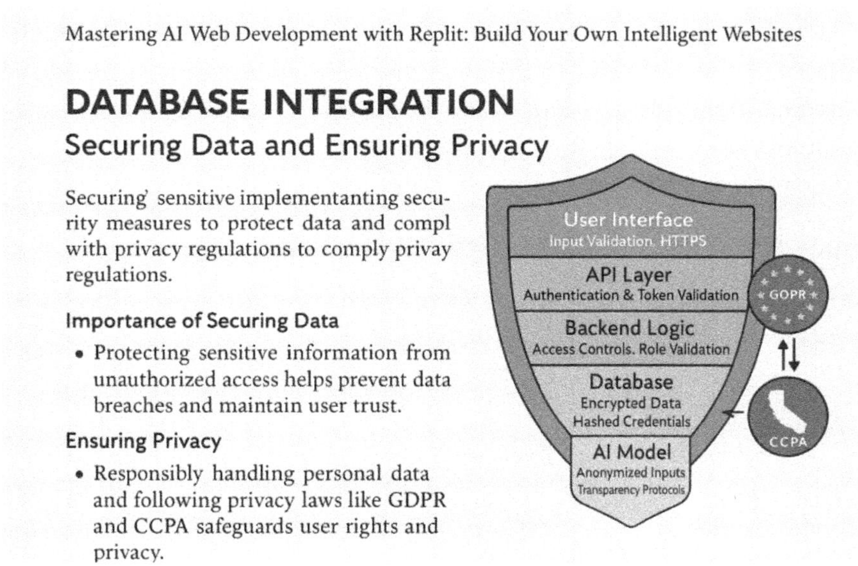

Final Thoughts

Security and privacy are not optional in modern web development. When integrating databases into AI-enabled websites, especially on platforms like Replit that streamline full-stack deployment, you must build security in from the start. Respect for user data is not just a technical concern - it's a moral and strategic imperative.

Chapter 9: Integrating Payment Methods

Overview of Payment Gateway Options

When building intelligent websites, especially those involving e-commerce, digital subscriptions, or AI-powered services, payment integration becomes a critical component.

What Is a Payment Gateway?

A **payment gateway** is a technology that securely transmits payment data from the customer to the acquiring bank. It serves as the bridge between the user's payment method and your application. When you collect payments, the gateway handles the sensitive information, ensuring compliance with financial regulations and security protocols.

Key Criteria for Selecting a Payment Gateway

When choosing a gateway to integrate into your intelligent website, consider:

- **Ease of Integration**: Developer-friendly APIs and SDKs
- **Security**: PCI-DSS compliance, encryption standards
- **Supported Payment Methods**: Credit cards, digital wallets, bank transfers
- **Global Reach**: Currency and country support
- **Fees and Pricing**: Transaction fees, setup costs, and chargeback handling
- **AI/Automation Features**: Fraud detection, smart invoicing, or user analytics

Popular Payment Gateway Options

1. Stripe

- **Best for**: Developers and startups
- **Features**: Clean RESTful API, smart fraud detection (Radar), recurring payments, one-click checkout
- **Replit Compatibility**: Works well with Node.js or Python backend using stripe library
- **Extras**: Built-in support for subscriptions, invoicing, and dynamic 3D Secure

Code Example (Python):

```
import stripe

import os


stripe.api_key = os.getenv("STRIPE_SECRET_KEY")


session = stripe.checkout.Session.create(

    payment_method_types=['card'],

    line_items=[{

        'price_data': {

            'currency': 'usd',

            'product_data': {'name': 'AI Chatbot Subscription'},

            'unit_amount': 1000,

        },
```

```
        'quantity': 1,
    }],
    mode='payment',
    success_url='https://your-app.repl.co/success',
    cancel_url='https://your-app.repl.co/cancel',
)
```

2. PayPal

- **Best for**: Rapid deployment and customer trust
- **Features**: Express checkout, PayPal Wallet, credit/debit card payments
- **Replit Compatibility**: REST API via SDKs (Python, Node.js)
- **Extras**: Buyer protection and dispute management built-in

3. Square

- **Best for**: Physical + online hybrid businesses
- **Features**: Payment APIs, POS integration, subscriptions, invoicing
- **Replit Compatibility**: Works through server-side APIs
- **Extras**: Advanced inventory and sales reporting

4. Razorpay (for India-based Users)

- **Best for**: Indian startups and local currency support
- **Features**: UPI, Netbanking, wallets, recurring billing
- **Replit Compatibility**: REST API and client-side JavaScript SDK

5. Braintree

- **Best for**: Full-stack payment systems with PayPal and Venmo integration
- **Features**: Vaulting, recurring billing, mobile-friendly checkout
- **Replit Compatibility**: Supports server SDKs in Python and Node.js

Key Security Practices

- Use **HTTPS** for all payment interactions.
- Store **payment-related environment variables** securely using Replit's Secrets feature.
- Never handle raw credit card data on your server unless you are PCI-DSS certified.
- Use **webhooks** to receive transaction status and updates from the payment provider.

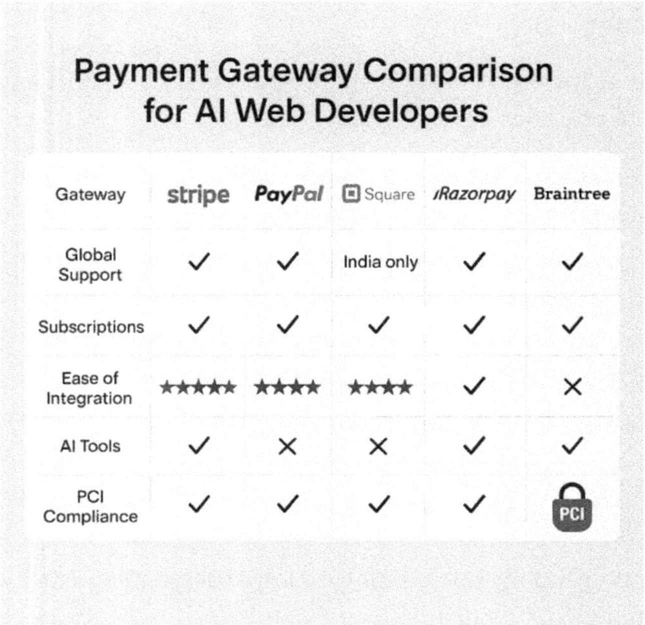

Title: "Payment Gateway Comparison for AI Web Developers"

Visual Design:

A table-style infographic comparing 5 popular gateways (Stripe, PayPal, Square, Razorpay, Braintree) across key features:

Gateway	Global Support	Subscriptions	Ease of Integration	AI Tools	PCI Compliance
Stripe	✓	✓	★★★★★	✓	✓
PayPal	✓	✓	★★★★	✕	✓
Square	✓ (limited)	✓	★★★★	✕	✓

Gateway	Global Support	Subscriptions	Ease of Integration	AI Tools	PCI Compliance
Razorpay	India only	✓	⭐⭐⭐⭐	✕	✓
Braintree	✓	✓	⭐⭐⭐⭐	✓	✓

Extras:

- Visual icons for each provider.
- PCI badge and a lock icon emphasizing security.
- Arrows pointing to integration examples on Replit (Node.js, Python).

Final Thoughts

Integrating the right payment gateway can significantly impact user trust, conversion rates, and overall experience. Stripe is often the go-to for developers due to its flexibility and developer-first tooling. However, your choice should align with your user base, region, and business goals.

Tip: Test in sandbox environments before going live. Monitor transactions using webhooks and logs inside Replit to debug payment flows in real time.

Setting Up Payment APIs

Secure, reliable payment processing is essential for any intelligent website that sells products, subscriptions, or credits. Replit makes it straightforward to wire popular providers into your project, but you still need a clear plan.

1. Foundations

1. **HTTPS first**
   Every payment flow must run over TLS. Replit automatically issues certificates for your .repl.co domain, so you can focus on code.

2. **Environment variables**
   Store all secrets in the **Secrets** tab. Example names:

```
STRIPE_SECRET_KEY

PAYPAL_CLIENT_ID

PAYPAL_CLIENT_SECRET

STRIPE_WEBHOOK_SECRET
```

3. **Webhook exposure**
   Use Replit's public URL during development; in production point your DNS record to Replit so the gateway can reach /webhook.

2. Stripe Quick-Start (Python + Flask)

Install libraries

```
poetry add stripe flask python-dotenv
```

Create checkout session

```
# app.py

import os, stripe, json

from flask import Flask, request, jsonify

stripe.api_key = os.getenv("STRIPE_SECRET_KEY")


app = Flask(__name__)
```

```
@app.post("/create-checkout-session")
def create_checkout():
    session = stripe.checkout.Session.create(
        payment_method_types=["card"],
        line_items=[{
            "price_data": {
                "currency": "usd",
                "unit_amount": 1000,
                "product_data": {"name": "Pro AI Subscription"},
            },
            "quantity": 1,
        }],
        mode="payment",
        success_url=request.host_url + "success",
        cancel_url=request.host_url + "cancel",
    )
    return jsonify({"url": session.url})
```

Verify payments in a webhook

```
@app.post("/webhook")
def stripe_webhook():
    payload = request.data
```

```
    sig = request.headers.get("Stripe-Signature")
    event = stripe.Webhook.construct_event(
        payload, sig, os.getenv("STRIPE_WEBHOOK_SECRET"))
    if event["type"] == "checkout.session.completed":
        session = event["data"]["object"]
        # mark order paid in DB
    return "", 200
```

Test flow

1. stripe login and stripe listen --forward-to localhost:5000/webhook
2. Use test card 4242 4242 4242 4242 for sandbox transactions.

3. PayPal Quick-Start (Node.js + Express)

Install libraries

```
npm i @paypal/checkout-server-sdk express dotenv
```

Server configuration

```
// server.js
require("dotenv").config();
const express = require("express");
const { PayPalHttpClient, SandboxEnvironment } = require("@paypal/checkout-server-sdk");
const app = express();

const environment = new SandboxEnvironment(
```

```
  process.env.PAYPAL_CLIENT_ID,
  process.env.PAYPAL_CLIENT_SECRET
);
const client = new PayPalHttpClient(environment);

app.post("/create-order", async (_, res) => {
  const request = {
    intent: "CAPTURE",
    purchase_units: [{ amount: { value: "10.00", currency_code:
"USD" } }]
  };
  const order = await client.execute({ path: "/v2/checkout/orders",
method: "post", body: request });
  res.json({ id: order.result.id });
});

app.post("/capture-order/:id", async (req, res) => {
  const capture = await client.execute({ path:
`/v2/checkout/orders/${req.params.id}/capture`, method: "post"
});
  // record payment in DB
  res.json(capture.result);
});
```

Client integration

Include PayPal's JS SDK script:

```
<script src="https://www.paypal.com/sdk/js?client-id=YOUR_CLIENT_ID"></script>

<div id="paypal-button-container"></div>

<script>

paypal.Buttons({

  createOrder: () => fetch("/create-order",{method:"post"}).then(r=>r.json()).then(o=>o.id),

  onApprove: d => fetch(`/capture-order/${d.orderID}`,{method:"post"})

}).render("#paypal-button-container");

</script>
```

4. Common Patterns and Gotchas

Concern	Stripe	PayPal	Why it matters
Live vs test keys	Prefixed sk_test_ / sk_live_	Sandbox vs live apps	Prevent accidental real charges during dev
Idempotency	Idempotency-Key header	Automatic retries built-in	Avoid duplicate orders on

Concern	Stripe	PayPal	Why it matters
			network hiccups
Currency support	135+	25+	Match your market
Fraud tools	Radar	Seller Protection	Reduce chargebacks
Refund API	stripe.Refund.create	/v2/payments/captures/{id}/refund	Automate support workflows

5. Security Checklist

- Validate webhook signatures every time.
- Never log raw card numbers or CVVs.
- Use strict CORS rules so only your domain can hit payment endpoints.
- Apply rate limiting on /create-checkout-session and /create-order.

6. Beyond Stripe and PayPal

Square, Razorpay, Braintree, and Adyen follow the same rhythm: create a checkout token, redirect or embed a widget, listen for a webhook, update your database, and send confirmations. Once you master one gateway, porting to another is usually a matter of swapping SDK calls and keys.

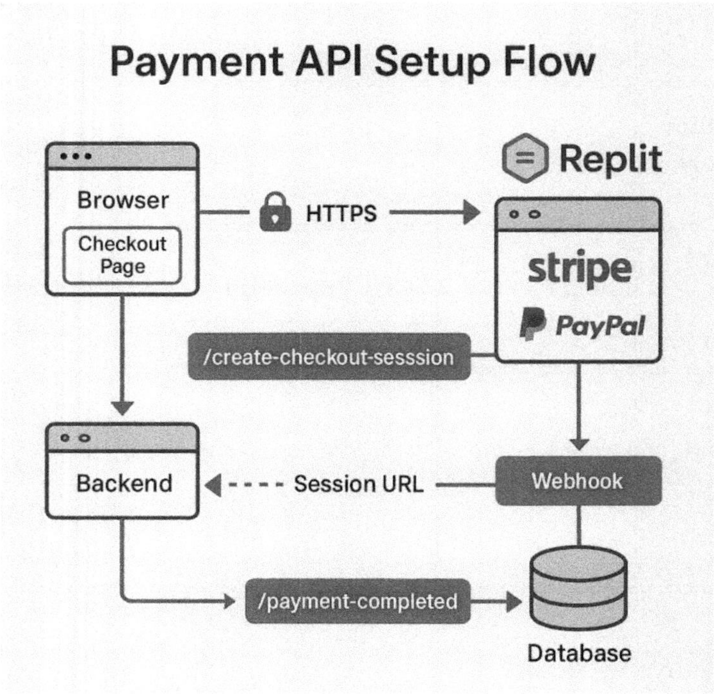

Implementing Secure Transactions

Handling money online is an attractive target for attackers. A single lapse can expose card data, cause fraud, or violate PCI-DSS. This section shows how to lock down every stage of a transaction in a Replit-hosted app.

1. Encrypt the Pipe

Layer	Action
Transport	Replit issues TLS certs automatically; force HTTPS with a 301 in your framework and enable HSTS (max-age=31536000; includeSubDomains).
Internal calls	When your backend talks to micro-services, still use HTTPS or mutual-TLS tunnels.

2. Never Touch Raw Card Data

Use **tokenization**. Stripe Elements, Stripe Checkout, PayPal Smart Buttons, and Braintree Hosted Fields send card numbers straight to the provider. Your JavaScript receives only a **token** or **payment-method ID**, which you forward to the server.

```
// Stripe client side

const {token} = await stripe.createToken(cardElement);

await fetch("/pay", {method:"POST",
body:JSON.stringify({token})});
```

Your server then creates a charge:

```
charge = stripe.Charge.create(

  amount=1000, currency="usd",

  source=request.json["token"], description="Pro plan")
```

3. Verify Webhooks Safely

1. Keep a secret per environment (STRIPE_WEBHOOK_SECRET).
2. Reconstruct the signature.

```
payload = request.data

sig_header = request.headers["Stripe-Signature"]

event = stripe.Webhook.construct_event(payload, sig_header, secret)
```

3. Check event["type"], mark orders paid, and respond 200 within 10 s.

4. Apply the Principle of Least Privilege

- **API keys**. Store each gateway key in Replit Secrets. Rotate quarterly.
- **Database roles**. A webhook handler needs only UPDATE payments, not full admin.
- **Firewall**. Allow inbound traffic to /webhook only from the gateway's IP ranges or use an HMAC header validated before any DB hit.

5. Prevent Fraud in Real Time

Tactic	**Stripe**	**PayPal**	**Implementation**
Address Verification (AVS)	✓	✓	Require billing_details.address at checkout.
CVV check	✓	✓	Enabled by default.
3-D Secure / SCA	Dynamic	Smart Payment Buttons	Force 3-D Secure if risk_level == "elevated".
Velocity limits	Radar Rules	N/A	Block > 3 attempts / minute / IP.

Add reCAPTCHA or hCAPTCHA before /create-checkout-session to slow bots.

6. Secure Logging and Monitoring

- Mask tokens and PII in logs. Example: replace middle digits of card IDs with ••••.
- Ship logs to a provider that supports log-level encryption at rest.
- Alert on: repeated declined charges, webhook failures, auth errors.

7. Idempotency and Race Conditions

Gateways may retry webhook posts. Guard your DB writes:

```
def record_payment(session_id, amount):
    if db.payments.find_one({"session_id":session_id}):
        return  # already processed
    db.payments.insert_one({"session_id":session_id,
"amount":amount})
```

Stripe offers an Idempotency-Key header so duplicate API calls do not double-charge.

8. Compliance Checklist

- PCI-DSS SAQ-A: qualifies because card data never hits your server.
- GDPR / CCPA: delete tokens upon user request; store only minimal metadata.
- PSD2: ensure Strong Customer Authentication for EU cards.
- SOC 2: log retention and access reviews.

9. Disaster-Proof Your Secrets

1. Encrypt a backup of .env and store it in a separate cloud vault.
2. Use Replit's secret history to roll back accidental changes.
3. Automate revocation. If GitHub push contains a key string, run stripe api-keys rotate.

10. Put It All Together

Follow this run-order every time a customer pays:

1. Browser loads provider-hosted fields, submits card.
2. Gateway returns a token.
3. Backend exchanges token for a charge.
4. Gateway sends a signed webhook.
5. Backend validates signature, writes immutable ledger row, emits receipt email.

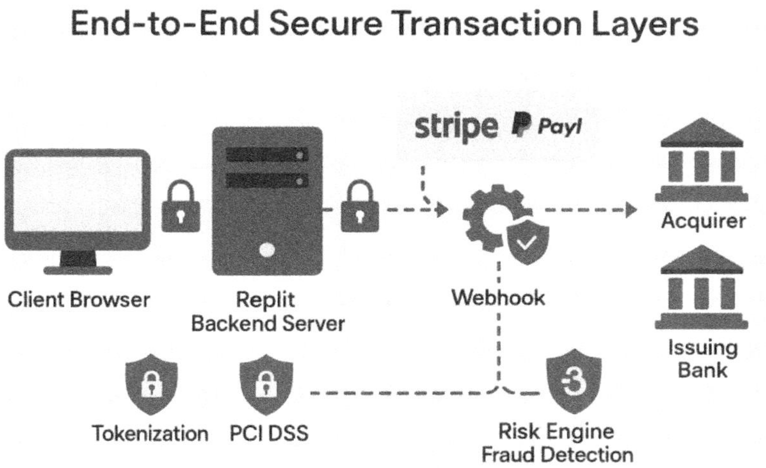

The diagram above shows every hop with encryption locks and shields so new team members can trace the trust boundaries at a glance.

Secure transactions are not an add-on. Build them into your project from the first commit and you will avoid costly rewrites, chargebacks, and regulatory fines later.

Managing Subscriptions and Recurring Payments

Subscriptions turn one-off customers into predictable revenue. Replit's always-on deployments pair perfectly with automated billing cycles, but only if you wire them correctly.

1. Subscription Building Blocks

Concept	Description
Product	The thing you sell, for example "Pro AI Plan".

Concept	Description
Price / Plan	Currency, amount, billing interval (monthly, yearly), trial length.
Customer	Stores payment method and billing info.
Subscription	Ties a customer to a price. Renews until canceled.
Webhook	Gateway-to-server callback that reports lifecycle events.

2. Stripe in Practice (Python + Flask)

a. Define products and prices

Create once in the Stripe dashboard or via API:

price_id = "price_1Oz1ABXYZ"

b. Checkout with a trial

```
@app.post("/begin-subscription")
def begin():
    session = stripe.checkout.Session.create(
        mode="subscription",
        line_items=[{"price": price_id, "quantity": 1}],
        customer_email=request.json["email"],
        subscription_data={"trial_period_days": 7},

success_url=f"{BASE}/thanks?session={{CHECKOUT_SESSION
_ID}}",
```

```
        cancel_url=f"{BASE}/cancel",
    )
    return jsonify({"url": session.url})
```

c. Handle renewals and status changes

```
@app.post("/stripe-webhook")
def stripe_webhook():
    event = verify_webhook(request)  # signature check omitted for brevity
    data = event["data"]["object"]

    if event["type"] == "invoice.payment_succeeded":
        db.subs.update_one({"id": data["subscription"]},
                           {"$set": {"status": "active"}})

    if event["type"] == "invoice.payment_failed":
        db.subs.update_one({"id": data["subscription"]},
                           {"$set": {"status": "past_due"}})

    if event["type"] == "customer.subscription.deleted":
        db.subs.update_one({"id": data["id"]},
                           {"$set": {"status": "canceled"}})
    return "", 200
```

d. Upgrades and downgrades with proration

```
stripe.Subscription.modify(
    sub_id,
    proration_behavior="create_prorations",
    items=[{"id": item_id, "price": new_price_id}],
)
```

Stripe calculates credit for unused time and charges or refunds the remainder automatically.

3. PayPal Parity

- Create a **Plan** with /v1/billing/plans (interval, amount, trial).
- Create a **Subscription** /v1/billing/subscriptions and capture approval URL.
- Listen to BILLING.SUBSCRIPTION.ACTIVATED, ...SUSPENDED, ...CANCELLED webhooks.
  The server-side bookkeeping mirrors the Stripe example.

4. Dealing With Failed Payments

1. **Retry schedule** – Stripe Smart Retries or PayPal's retry_time array.
2. **Grace period** – Flag account as past_due but keep features for 3–5 days.
3. **Dunning email** – "Your card expired. Update it to keep access."
4. **Automatic card updater** – Enabled by default on major card networks.

5. Metered Billing and Usage Records

For pay-as-you-go credits:

```
stripe.UsageRecord.create(
    quantity=api_calls,
    timestamp=int(time.time()),
    subscription_item=item_id,
    action="increment",
)
```

Invoices aggregate usage each period.

6. Analytics to Reduce Churn

Metric	Query idea
Net MRR	Sum(active_sub.amount) – refunds.
Churn rate	canceled_this_month / active_last_month.
Expansion MRR	Upgrades – downgrades.

Store subscription snapshots nightly. Display in a simple Replit chart or export to BigQuery.

7. Security and Compliance Checklist

- Store customer IDs only, never raw card data.
- Protect /stripe-webhook with signature and a random path such as /whk/5f3e....
- Enforce one subscription per user to avoid duplicate charges.
- Honor GDPR delete requests by first canceling the subscription, then deleting the customer.

8. Migration Tips

- Import existing subscribers via Stripe's **Customer Import** CSV tool.
- Map legacy plan IDs to new price IDs in a translation table.
- Run dual webhooks during cut-over for zero downtime.

9. When to Cancel Automatically

Trigger	Action
3 failed retries	Downgrade to free tier.
User deletion	Cancel immediately with invoice_now=true.
Abuse detection	Suspend subscription and refund last charge if appropriate.

10. Recap

Subscriptions require more moving parts than one-time payments. Automate everything – creation, renewal, upgrade, downgrade, and cancellation – then monitor events through webhooks to keep your database in sync.

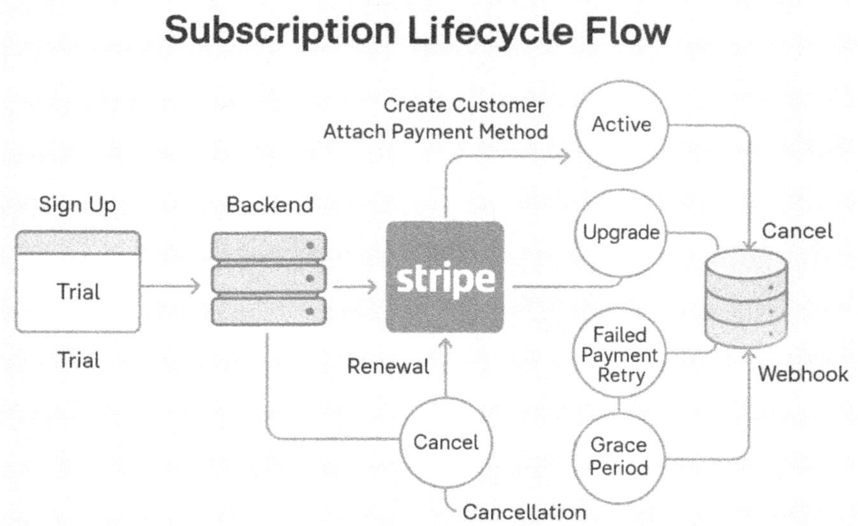

The diagram above shows each state and how Stripe, your backend, and webhooks interact, giving you an at-a-glance reference for onboarding new developers.

Implement these patterns once and your Replit-hosted SaaS can scale from your first customer to thousands without billing headaches.

Testing and Debugging Payment Systems

When working with real money, testing is more than just best practice - it is essential. Faulty payment logic can result in lost revenue, double charges, failed renewals, or compliance violations.

1. Understand the Payment Testing Environment

Both Stripe and PayPal offer full-featured **sandbox modes** where you can simulate real-world behavior using test API keys and dummy payment methods.

Gateway	Test Mode	Endpoint Behavior
Stripe	sk_test_ keys	Simulates real transactions, cards, failures
PayPal	Sandbox App	Simulated buyer/seller logins

Replit Integration Tip

Use Replit's **Secrets Manager** to switch between test and live keys. For example:

import os

stripe.api_key = os.getenv("STRIPE_SECRET_KEY") # store sk_test_... or sk_live_...

2. Simulating Transactions in Stripe

Use their test card numbers:

- 4242 4242 4242 4242: Successful transaction
- 4000 0000 0000 9995: Declined card
- 4000 0000 0000 0341: 3D Secure required
- Use any future expiry date, any CVC (e.g. 123)

Example test request:

```
curl -X POST https://api.stripe.com/v1/charges \
  -u sk_test_...: \
  -d amount=2000 \
  -d currency=usd \
  -d source=tok_visa \
```

-d description="Test Charge"

3. Testing Webhooks

Payment gateways notify your app using webhooks. On Replit:

- Make sure your Repl is **public**.
- Expose a route like /webhook to receive Stripe or PayPal events.

To simulate webhook events:

stripe login

stripe listen --forward-to localhost:5000/webhook

stripe trigger checkout.session.completed

Test for event types like:

- invoice.payment_succeeded
- invoice.payment_failed
- customer.subscription.deleted

Always **verify the signature** of webhook requests using the secret from your dashboard.

4. Common Bugs and Debugging Techniques

Bug	**Symptom**	**Fix**
Duplicate charges	Customer charged twice	Use Idempotency-Key header for all write operations

Bug	Symptom	Fix
Webhook not firing	Subscription created but no backend update	Check event type filtering or URL accessibility
Currency mismatch	Payments fail for some cards	Ensure correct currency when creating the price object
Checkout doesn't redirect	Blank page or error	Ensure your success_url and cancel_url are HTTPS and hosted

Use logging extensively:

```
@app.post("/webhook")
def webhook():
    log_event = request.data
    with open("logs.txt", "a") as log:
        log.write(log_event.decode() + "\n")
    return "", 200
```

5. Testing in PayPal Sandbox

- Go to developer.paypal.com
- Create sandbox test accounts (Buyer and Merchant)
- Use buyer credentials in the browser pop-up
- Listen to webhooks at /paypal-webhook and simulate events

PayPal also allows programmatic testing of failed payments by using sandbox states like:

- Payment denied
- Subscription expired
- Refund issued

6. Use Case Walkthrough: Testing Subscription Renewal

1. Create a product and plan with a **1-minute interval** (only allowed in test mode).
2. Subscribe a test customer.
3. Wait for first payment.
4. Stripe auto-renews after 1 minute and triggers invoice.paid again.
5. Verify logs and database changes.
6. Cancel subscription and confirm customer.subscription.deleted webhook.

7. Automating Tests in Replit

You can script some of your tests using pytest, unittest, or Postman collections:

- Mock the Stripe API using Stripe-mock
- Use a test database (e.g., SQLite or MongoDB memory server)
- Inject fake webhooks during integration testing

Example with pytest:

def test_webhook(client):

fake_event = {"type": "checkout.session.completed", "data": {"object": {"id": "test"}}}

res = client.post("/webhook", json=fake_event)

assert res.status_code == 200

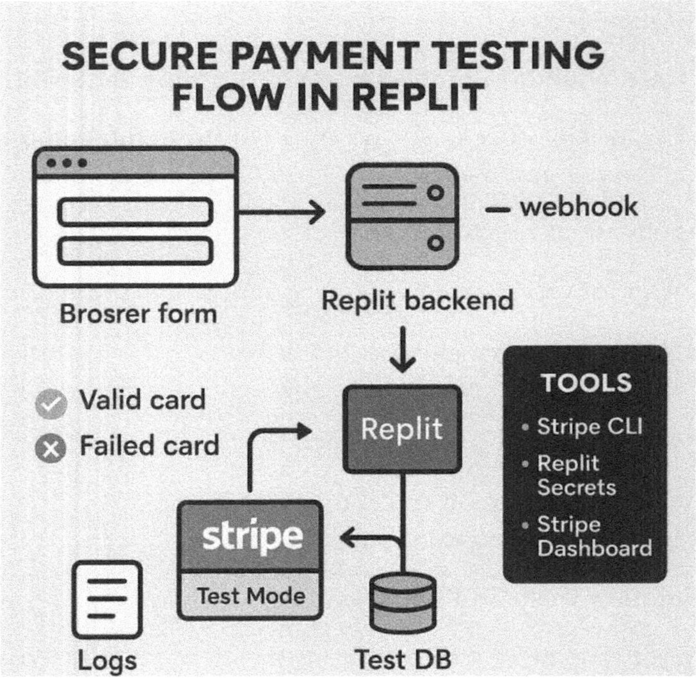

8. Visualizing the Flow

[Illustration: Payment Testing & Debugging Flow]

Title: "Secure Payment Testing Flow in Replit"

Visual layout:

- Browser form (test card entry) → Replit backend
- Arrows:

- ✓ Valid card → Stripe Test Mode
- ✗ Failed card → Decline handler

- Stripe (or PayPal) triggers webhook → /webhook route
- Logs file and test DB update shown
- Sidebox with "Tools": Stripe CLI, Replit Secrets, Stripe Dashboard

Testing and debugging payment systems on Replit requires discipline, structure, and a test-first mindset. Treat the sandbox as a staging ground for all edge cases: retries, failures, expirations, upgrades, downgrades, and cancellations. Build reusable logs, simulate live environments with test users, and validate with CLI tools before shipping any production code.

Chapter 10: Connecting to External Domains

Registering a Domain Name

A custom domain name is not just a branding tool, it's a mark of credibility and control. If you're building intelligent web applications with Replit, connecting your project to a personal or business domain takes your project from a development sandbox to a polished, production-ready site.

1. What Is a Domain Name?

A **domain name** is your website's unique address on the internet, such as youraiapp.com. It is mapped to the IP address of your web server (or in our case, Replit-hosted project) via the Domain Name System (DNS).

2. Choosing and Registering a Domain

a. Pick a Name

- Keep it short, memorable, and relevant (e.g. airesumehelper.com)
- Avoid numbers and hyphens
- Use .com if possible, or relevant TLDs like .ai, .tech, .dev

b. Choose a Registrar

A **domain registrar** is a service that sells and manages domain names. Popular and reliable registrars include:

Registrar	**Pros**	**Notes**
Namecheap	Affordable, easy UI	Free WHOIS privacy
Google Domains (now under Squarespace)	Integrated with Google tools	Transparent pricing
GoDaddy	Wide selection, upsells a lot	Expensive renewals
Porkbun	Clean interface, low cost	Excellent support
Cloudflare	Cost price, DNS included	Requires account setup

Tip: Register your domain in your own account. Do not let clients or collaborators own critical infrastructure.

c. Search & Buy

Most registrars have a search bar. Once you find an available domain, you can:

- Add to cart
- Choose registration length (1–10 years)
- Enable auto-renew
- Enable WHOIS privacy protection (included by default in most services now)

3. Domain Ownership Essentials

After purchase:

- You are the **registrant** and domain **admin**
- You gain access to DNS settings (nameservers, records)
- You can transfer the domain later if needed

Registrars send confirmation and management links to your email. Keep it updated and secure with 2FA.

4. What You'll Need to Connect to Replit

Once your domain is registered, you'll connect it to your Replit-hosted project using:

- **CNAME** records (for subdomains like www.youraiapp.com)
- **A** records (for root domains like youraiapp.com, if needed)
- Access to your registrar's **DNS management** console

Replit provides domain connection instructions after you select "Custom Domain" in your project settings. You'll paste a verification record first, then point the domain to Replit's IP/CNAME target.

5. Optional: Email Setup

If you want email addresses like contact@youraiapp.com, you'll need:

- An email host (Google Workspace, Zoho Mail, Fastmail)
- MX records configured in your domain DNS
- SPF, DKIM, and DMARC records for spam protection

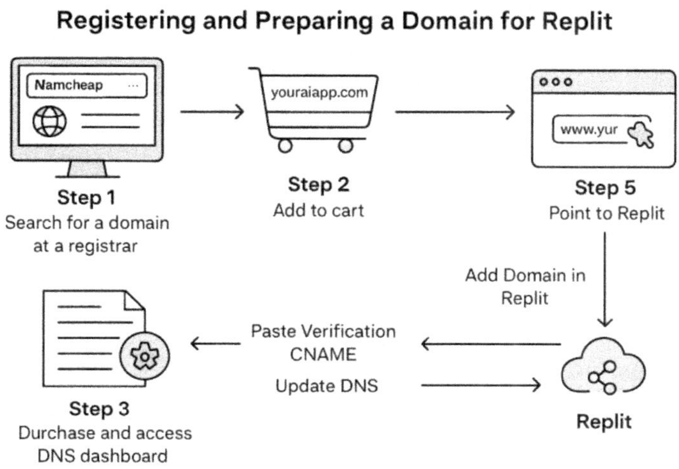

[Illustration: Domain Registration Flow]

Title: "Registering and Preparing a Domain for Replit"

Diagram layout:

1. **Step 1**: User browsing a registrar website (like Namecheap) and searching for a domain
2. **Step 2**: Shopping cart with a domain name
3. **Step 3**: Purchase confirmation and DNS dashboard access
4. **Step 4**: Arrow pointing toward Replit with labels "Add Domain in Replit", "Paste Verification CNAME", "Update DNS"
5. **Step 5**: Browser icon pointing to www.youraiapp.com → Replit

Icons included: globe (domain), gear (DNS settings), padlock (WHOIS privacy), arrow to Replit cloud logo.

Registering a domain name is the first public commitment to your intelligent web app. It signals professionalism, builds trust, and opens the door to a consistent online identity. With just a few steps, your Replit-hosted app can live under a sleek, custom address - ready for users, clients, and search engines.

Configuring DNS Settings

Once you have successfully registered a domain name, the next step in publishing your intelligent website from Replit under a custom domain is configuring the **DNS (Domain Name System)** settings. This configuration determines how traffic is routed from the domain name to your Replit-hosted project.

1. Understanding DNS Basics

DNS records are instructions that tell the internet how to route domain traffic. The most important types when connecting to Replit are:

Record Type	Purpose
A	Points a domain to an IP address (e.g., 34.123.45.67)
CNAME	Points a subdomain to another domain (e.g., yourapp.com → cname.repl.co)
TXT	Typically used for verification and security (e.g., Google verification, SPF for email)

Note: Replit primarily uses **CNAME records** for domain verification and hosting.

2. Accessing DNS Settings

After purchasing your domain, log in to your domain registrar and access the **DNS Management** or **Zone Editor** section. The interface varies by provider, but you'll typically see a table of existing records.

3. Adding DNS Records for Replit

When you open the **"Custom Domain"** section in your Replit project, you'll be provided with:

- A **verification CNAME** record
- A **target host** (usually something like cname.vercel-dns.com or Replit's specific alias)

Example for www.youraiapp.com:

Type	Name	Value
CNAME	www	cname.replit.com.

Steps:

1. Delete any existing A or AAAA records for the root or subdomain.
2. Add a new **CNAME** record:
   - Name/Host: www
   - Value: cname.replit.com (or the address Replit gives)
3. Save changes.

4. Optional: Forwarding Root Domain

DNS does not allow a CNAME on the root domain (youraiapp.com). To redirect traffic from the root to www.youraiapp.com:

- Use your registrar's **URL forwarding** option if available.
- Or use a third-party DNS provider like Cloudflare that supports **flattened CNAMEs** or page rules.

5. Propagation and Verification

DNS changes may take time to propagate globally—up to **24–48 hours**, but usually less than an hour.

After updating your DNS, return to Replit:

- Enter your domain under "Custom Domain"
- Click **Verify and Connect**
- Replit will check the DNS status and link your project once the record is live

6. Troubleshooting Common Issues

Problem	Cause	Fix
"Domain not verified"	CNAME hasn't propagated yet	Wait and retry in 10–30 mins
403 or blank page	Record points to old IP or host	Ensure only the CNAME is set
Email not working	DNS records overwritten	Add MX, SPF, and DKIM for mail separately

7. Keeping DNS Secure

- **Lock your domain** to prevent unauthorized transfers
- **Enable 2FA** on your registrar account
- Avoid exposing unnecessary TXT records publicly

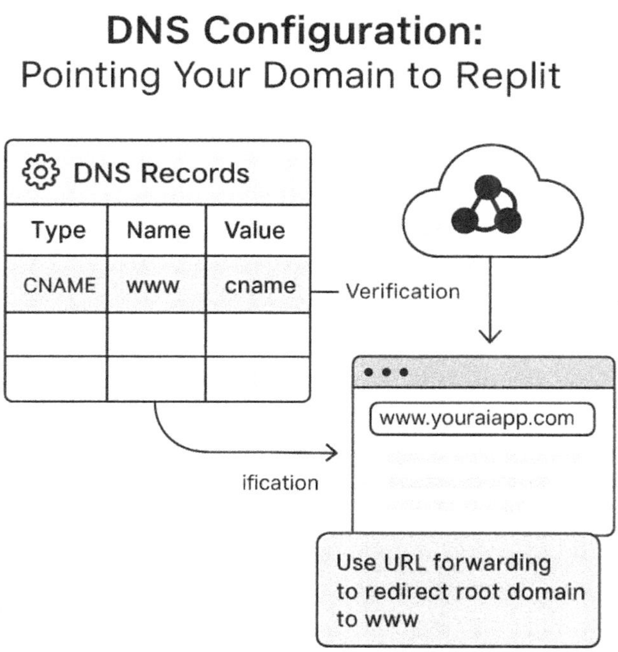

[Illustration: DNS Configuration for Replit Hosting]

Title: "DNS Configuration: Pointing Your Domain to Replit"

Diagram elements:

1. A registrar dashboard interface with a DNS Records table
2. Highlighted row showing:
    - Type: CNAME

    - Name: www
    - Value: cname.replit.com

3. Arrow labeled "Verification" pointing from DNS to Replit
4. Replit cloud icon with a live webpage preview (www.youraiapp.com)
5. Sidebar note: "Use URL forwarding to redirect root domain to www"

Properly configuring DNS settings is essential to make your intelligent website live under your chosen domain. DNS is often misunderstood, but once you grasp how CNAME and A records work, managing your domain becomes straightforward. With Replit handling the backend, all you need is correct DNS configuration to deliver your AI-powered web application to the world.

Linking Your Domain to Replit Projects

Once you've registered your domain name and configured your DNS records, the final step is to link your domain directly to your Replit project. This allows visitors to access your intelligent website using your branded URL (e.g. www.youraiapp.com) rather than a Replit subdomain (e.g. youraiapp.replit.app).

1. Why Link a Custom Domain?

- **Professionalism**: Builds trust with users and clients
- **Branding**: Promotes consistent visual identity
- **SEO**: Improves visibility and indexing
- **Persistence**: Your app stays recognizable even if you rebuild it later

2. Requirements Before You Begin

Before linking a domain:

- Make sure your DNS records (especially CNAME) are correctly configured
- Ensure your Replit project is **public** (or hosted on a paid plan for private domains)
- Allow 15–30 minutes for DNS propagation (or check live with tools like dnschecker.org)

3. Steps to Link a Custom Domain in Replit

a. Open Your Replit Project

1. Navigate to your project
2. Click the **"Tools"** panel on the left
3. Select **"Custom Domain"**

b. Enter Your Domain

- Input your domain (e.g. www.youraiapp.com)
- Click **"Add"**
  Replit will now scan your DNS configuration.

c. Copy the Verification Record (if prompted)

If Replit can't verify ownership automatically:

- You'll be given a **CNAME verification record**
- Go to your domain registrar's DNS settings
- Add the record under "Custom DNS" or "Advanced DNS"
- Recheck in Replit by clicking **"Verify"**

d. Connect and Deploy

Once verified:

- Replit links your domain and enables HTTPS automatically

- You'll see a message: ✅ **Your domain is live**

Example

If your domain is www.intellibot.dev and your Replit project is called intellibot, linking it will serve your AI app under https://www.intellibot.dev with TLS encryption via Replit's managed certificate.

4. Multiple Domains or Subdomains

You can add:

- www.yoursite.com
- app.yoursite.com
- beta.yoursite.ai

Each must be added and verified separately within Replit's domain tool.

If your registrar supports **wildcard CNAMEs**, you may also route all subdomains to the same project (e.g., *.yoursite.com).

5. Replacing the Replit Default Domain

After linking a custom domain:

- The Replit subdomain still works (e.g. youraiapp.replit.app)
- You can set up **301 redirects** at the Replit app level (optional)
- Prefer your custom domain in marketing, documentation, and SEO

6. Maintenance Tips

Task	Frequency
Renew your domain	Yearly or auto-renew
Re-verify DNS if settings change	As needed
Check HTTPS status	After 24 hrs or DNS change
Backup DNS config	Every quarter or after edits

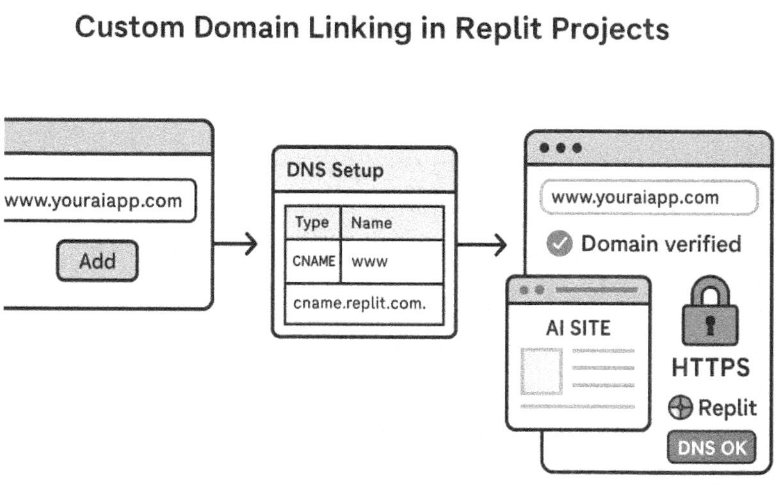

[Illustration: Linking Your Domain to Replit]

Title: "Custom Domain Linking in Replit Projects"

Visual Layout:

- **Step 1**: Screenshot-style panel with Replit's "Custom Domain" input form

- **Step 2**: Arrow pointing to DNS setup box showing sample CNAME record
- **Step 3**: Green checkmark appearing on Replit UI ("Domain Verified")
- **Step 4**: Browser showing www.youraiapp.com loading your AI site
- Sidebar: TLS padlock, HTTPS, Replit logo, and "DNS OK" tag

Replit's custom domain support removes much of the hassle traditionally involved in web hosting. With just a domain and a few DNS tweaks, your AI-powered application can go from prototype to production under your own domain name. Take care to verify, monitor, and document your DNS settings so your users always have uninterrupted access.

SSL Certificates and Secure Connections

HTTPS is no longer optional. Modern browsers flag insecure sites, search engines demote them, and many APIs reject plain HTTP. When you link a custom domain to a Replit project, you must understand how Transport Layer Security (TLS) and SSL certificates work, even though Replit automates most of the heavy lifting.

1. What a Certificate Does

1. **Encryption** – TLS encrypts traffic between the client and your server, protecting login credentials, payment tokens, and AI model responses from eavesdropping.
2. **Authentication** – The certificate chain proves that www.youraiapp.com is really your site and not an impostor.
3. **Integrity** – The handshake guarantees that packets are not tampered with in transit.

A certificate is essentially a signed file containing your public key, domain name, expiry date, and the signature of a trusted Certificate Authority (CA).

2. Replit's Automatic HTTPS

- When you host on the default *.replit.app subdomain, Replit issues a free Let's Encrypt certificate automatically.
- When you connect a **custom domain**, Replit:
    1. Creates or renews a Let's Encrypt cert for that domain.
    2. Installs the cert on its load balancer.
    3. Redirects all HTTP requests to HTTPS with a 301 status.

Renewals happen transparently every 60 days, so you never have to run cron jobs or scripts.

3. Certificate Lifecycle for a Custom Domain

Phase	What Happens
Validation	Let's Encrypt must prove you own the domain. Replit places a unique CNAME or HTTP-01 token.
Issuance	Once the CA verifies the token, it signs a certificate valid for 90 days.
Installation	Replit attaches the cert and private key to your project's edge proxy.
Renewal	At 60 days Replit repeats validation and swaps in a new cert before the old one expires.

If validation fails (for example a broken CNAME), Replit shows a red warning in the Custom Domain panel. Fix DNS and click "Retry validation".

4. Upgrading Security Settings

1. **HSTS** – Add a header in your web framework:

```
from flask import Flask, make_response


app = Flask(__name__)


@app.after_request
def hsts(response):
    response.headers["Strict-Transport-Security"] = "max-age=63072000; includeSubDomains"
    return response
```

2. **OCSP Stapling** – Handled by Replit's reverse proxy.
3. **TLS 1.3** – Enabled by default. No action required.
4. **HTTP → HTTPS redirect** – Replit does this automatically for custom domains. For extra safety, add a client-side meta redirect in your <head>.

5. Mixed-Content Pitfalls

If you embed external scripts or images over http:// your page will break on modern browsers. Always:

- Use https:// for all CDN links.
- Prefer protocol-relative URLs (//cdn.example.com/...) only if the CDN supports HTTPS.

6. Testing Your Certificate

Tool	Purpose
SSL Labs (ssllabs.com/ssltest)	Deep scan of cipher suites and chain. Aim for grade A.
Security Headers (securityheaders.com)	Checks HSTS, CSP, and other headers.
Chrome DevTools	Under Security tab verify "Connection is secure".

7. Handling Multiple Domains and Wildcards

- Replit can issue certs for each subdomain you add (app.yoursite.com, api.yoursite.com). Add and verify them one at a time.
- Wildcard certificates (*.yoursite.com) are not yet supported directly. Instead, point each required subdomain via a CNAME and let Replit provision separate certs.

8. Disaster Recovery

1. Export your DNS zone file after every change.
2. Keep an off-platform status page that lives on another provider in case Replit outage affects TLS termination.
3. If you must migrate, you can re-use the same Let's Encrypt validation method on a new host with zero downtime by lowering TTL to 300 seconds the day before.

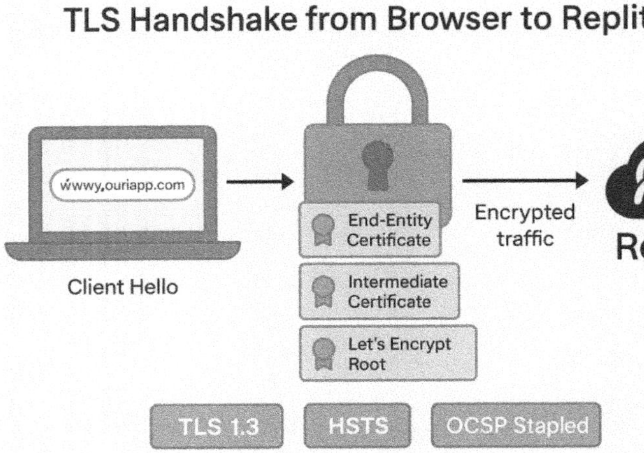

Illustration. "TLS Handshake From Browser to Replit"

Layout

- **Left**: Laptop icon with address bar https://www.youraiapp.com
- **Arrow 1**: "Client Hello" pointing to padlock
- **Center**: Padlock overlay showing certificate chain (End-Entity ▶ Intermediate ▶ Let's Encrypt Root)
- **Arrow 2**: "Encrypted traffic" pointing to Replit cloud icon
- **Bottom strip**: Green badges "TLS 1.3", "HSTS", "OCSP Stapled"

Troubleshooting Domain Connection Issues

Even with careful setup, custom-domain links sometimes fail. The flowchart below summarizes a systematic path to isolate the fault. Below is a deeper checklist you can apply when Verify in Replit shows red or your browser still resolves to the old site.

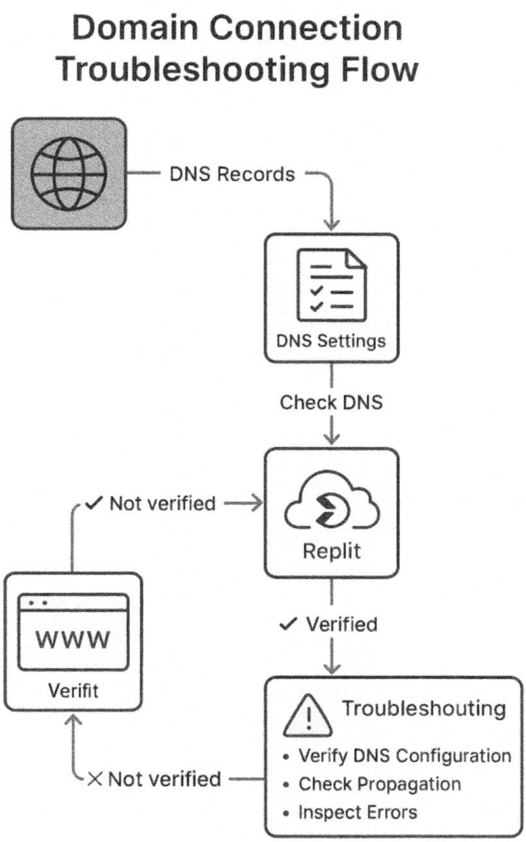

1 Check DNS Propagation First

Tool	What to look for
dnschecker.org	CNAME → cname.replit.com visible in most regions?
dig +trace www.youraiapp.com	Does the trace end at Replit's target?

Tool	What to look for
nslookup	No stale A/AAAA records left over on the root?

Fix: Remove stray A/AAAA, lower TTL to 300 s, wait up to 30 min.

2 Typical Error Messages & Root Causes

Symptom	Likely Cause	Remedy
Replit panel "Domain not verified"	Wrong record type or value	Copy CNAME exactly, no trailing spaces, ensure "@" is root only
Browser shows "404 Replit"	Domain resolves but no project mapped	Re-enter domain in **Custom Domain** tab and click *Connect*
SSL padlock missing	DNS recently changed	Wait for Let's Encrypt issuance (≤ 30 min) or retry validation
Redirect loop	Mixed HTTP & HTTPS on root vs **www**	Add one canonical CNAME, use registrar URL-forwarding for root
Works on mobile data, not on office Wi-Fi	ISP DNS cache	Flush local resolver or switch to 1.1.1.1 during testing

3 Step-by-Step Debug Routine

1. **dig cname** www.youraiapp.com **@1.1.1.1** – expect CNAME.
2. **curl -I** https://www.youraiapp.com – status 200 + server: replit header.
3. In Replit console run ping $REPLIT_DB_URL to ensure project is up.
4. Toggle the domain off/on in **Custom Domain** to force cert re-check.
5. Clear Cloudflare or other proxy caches if you use them.

4 Firewall & Proxy Interference

- Corporate proxies may strip CNAME flattening. Test via hotspot.
- Cloudflare "Orange-to-Orange" mode can break Let's Encrypt challenges - temporarily grey-cloud the CNAME during verification.

5 Logging & Monitoring

Bash in Replit shell to tail request logs

tail -f ~/logs/http.log | grep "youraiapp.com"

Look for Host header mismatches or 301 chains.

6 Automated Alerts

Set up a free UptimeRobot HTTPS check on your custom domain. Alert if status ❌ > 5 min; catch certificate expiry or DNS regressions early.

7 When All Else Fails

- Re-create the CNAME with a fresh random name provided by Replit.
- Open Replit Support with: domain, registrar, current DNS JSON from dig +nocmd +noall +answer.
- Roll back recent registrar DNS-template changes; some override CNAMEs silently.

With this checklist you can resolve 95 % of domain-connection issues in under an hour, keeping your AI-powered site reliably online.

Chapter 11: Step-by-Step Practice Projects

AI-driven Weather Forecast Website

This project shows how to combine a public weather API with an LLM to deliver friendly natural-language forecasts. Follow the five milestones below; you can complete the core build in an afternoon and iterate later.

Step	Goal	Key Tasks
1 Plan features	Decide UX and data scope	Real-time weather by city, 3-day forecast, AI summary, favourites list
2 Get a weather API	Pull raw meteorological data	OpenWeatherMap, WeatherAPI, or NOAA; generate an API key and store it in Replit Secrets
3 Build the site	Collect input and display JSON	Write a minimal HTML form. Use client-side fetch to call your own /weather?city= route; render temperature, humidity, icons
4 Add the AI layer	Summarise or translate data	In your backend hit the OpenAI / Gemini endpoint with a prompt like "Summarise these conditions for a casual reader"; return the text to the browser
5 Deploy and test	Push live on a custom domain	Link domain, confirm HTTPS, tail logs, add local-storage "star" button to save cities

```
# server.py (Flask)
from flask import Flask, request, jsonify
import os, requests, openai
app = Flask(__name__)
openai.api_key = os.getenv("OPENAI_KEY")
WX = os.getenv("WX_KEY")

@app.get("/weather")
def weather():
    city = request.args["city"]
    wx = requests.get(
        f"https://api.openweathermap.org/data/2.5/forecast",
        params={"q": city, "units": "metric", "appid": WX},
        timeout=10).json()
    return jsonify(wx)

@app.get("/ai-summary")
def ai():
    raw = request.args["data"]
    prompt = f"Give a friendly 3-sentence forecast: {raw}"
    out = openai.ChatCompletion.create(model="gpt-3.5-turbo",

messages=[{"role":"user","content":prompt}],
```

```
                        max_tokens=80)
    return out.choices[0].message.content.strip()
```

Testing checklist

- Use London then São Paulo to confirm UTF-8 handling.
- Simulate API downtime with wrong key; ensure graceful error.
- Lighthouse score ≥ 95 on mobile.

Ideas for stretch goals

- Auto-detect user location with the Geolocation API.
- Cache responses in Replit DB for 15 min to save tokens.
- Add speech synthesis so the forecast can be read aloud.

Step-by-Step Practice Projects

AI-driven Weather Forecast Website

Step 1 Plan Your Features

- Gather requirements: real–time weather data for a city; AI–generated forecast summary: favorite locations for quick access.

Step 2 Get a Weather API

- Set up an API key from someservice such as OpenWeather.

Step 3 Build the Website

- Use HTML and CSS for a simple UI design; Create a form to enter a city name Show forecast data and AI insights

```
async function fetchWeather(event) {
   event.preventbefaut(();
   const city = document.gletid('city'
   ".walue:
   conlt.response = awail fech(
      'https.//api.openweathmap.org/
      data/2.3/weather/q=3city)sappid=
      YOOR_APT_KEY"/
   )),
   const data = vait response.json;
   displayWeather(data);
   getaisummary(data);
}
```

Step 4 Integrate the AI Model

- Use the Openl API to generate a natural language summary of the weather

```
app.get("/ai-summary, asvic (req, res =>)
   const response = awalt
      openal.completion.crete(
      engine; "dpvinct",
      prompt: "Provide summary of
      the weather: $(req.queryq)`,
   max tokens: 60
   res.send(response.choices[@].text
trim));
```

Step 5 Deploy and Test

- Deploy applicattion to Replit: Add favorite locations with a Replit database

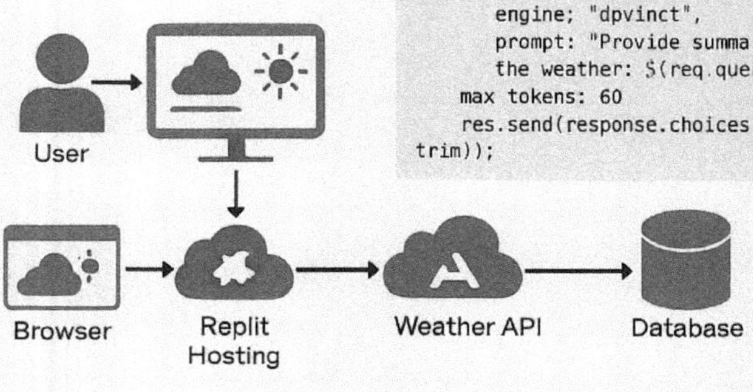

4

The diagram above maps the full data path: user → browser → Replit hosting → weather API → AI summary → browser, with an optional favourites database branch. Use it to orient newcomers before they dive into code.

Real-Time Sentiment Analysis App

Sentiment analysis is one of the most intuitive ways to apply AI to user-generated content. In this project, you'll build a web app that analyzes text in real time, classifies sentiment (positive, negative, neutral), and displays results instantly. This helps users understand tone - useful in emails, reviews, social media posts, or chatbot logs.

Project Overview

Feature	Description
Live text input	User enters or pastes text
Sentiment analysis	AI or NLP model evaluates tone
Visual feedback	Colored result and confidence score
Optional log	Recent analysis history stored locally

Step 1. Setup the Project

Create a new Replit project (Flask or Node.js) with the necessary front-end and back-end files.

Tech stack:

- Frontend: HTML, JavaScript, CSS
- Backend: Python (Flask) or Node.js (Express)
- AI API: OpenAI, Cohere, or Hugging Face

Install required libraries:

```
poetry add flask openai
```

Store your API key securely in the **Secrets** tab as OPENAI_API_KEY.

Step 2. Design the Frontend

Create a simple layout with:

```
<textarea id="user-input" placeholder="Type or paste text..."></textarea>

<button onclick="analyze()">Analyze Sentiment</button>

<div id="result"></div>
```

Add JavaScript to call your back-end API:

```
async function analyze() {
  const text = document.getElementById("user-input").value;
  const res = await fetch(`/analyze?text=${encodeURIComponent(text)}`);
  const data = await res.json();
  document.getElementById("result").innerHTML = `
    Sentiment: <b>${data.sentiment}</b> <br>
    Confidence: ${data.confidence}%
  `;
}
```

Step 3. Backend Sentiment Processing (OpenAI or Hugging Face)

Using OpenAI (ChatCompletion):

```
from flask import Flask, request, jsonify

import openai, os


app = Flask(__name__)

openai.api_key = os.getenv("OPENAI_API_KEY")


@app.route("/analyze")

def analyze():

    text = request.args.get("text", "")

    prompt = f"What is the sentiment of this sentence? Respond with Positive, Negative, or Neutral and a confidence score out of 100.\n\n{text}"

    res = openai.ChatCompletion.create(

        model="gpt-3.5-turbo",

        messages=[{"role": "user", "content": prompt}],

        max_tokens=50

    )

    reply = res.choices[0].message.content.strip()

    parts = reply.split()

    sentiment = parts[0]
```

```
    confidence = "".join(filter(str.isdigit, parts[-1])) or "?"
    return jsonify({"sentiment": sentiment, "confidence": confidence})
```

Step 4. Display Results with Styling

Use simple color cues:

```
#result {
  font-size: 1.2em;
  margin-top: 10px;
}
.positive { color: green; }
.negative { color: red; }
.neutral  { color: gray; }
```

Use JavaScript to add the class dynamically:

```
result.className = data.sentiment.toLowerCase();
```

Step 5. Real-Time Enhancements (Optional)

- Add input event listener to analyze as the user types (debounce required)
- Display emoji (😊 😐 😠) alongside results
- Maintain history in browser localStorage

Testing Checklist

Test Case	Expected Result
"I love this app!"	Positive, high confidence

Test Case	Expected Result
"It's okay I guess."	Neutral
"This is awful and broken."	Negative
Empty input	Skip or return warning

Advanced Stretch Goals

- Support batch input (analyze multiple sentences at once)
- Include emotion detection (happy, sad, angry, surprised)
- Graph results over time using Chart.js
- Create a browser extension version

Diagram: Real-Time Sentiment Flow

Title: "Real-Time Sentiment Analysis Flow in Replit"

Diagram layout:

1. **User types text →** textarea in browser
2. **Fetch call to /analyze →** Flask backend
3. **Backend calls OpenAI or NLP model API**
4. **API returns classification + confidence**
5. **Backend returns JSON to frontend**
6. **Frontend updates display with colored sentiment and emoji**
7. (Optional): Save result to history

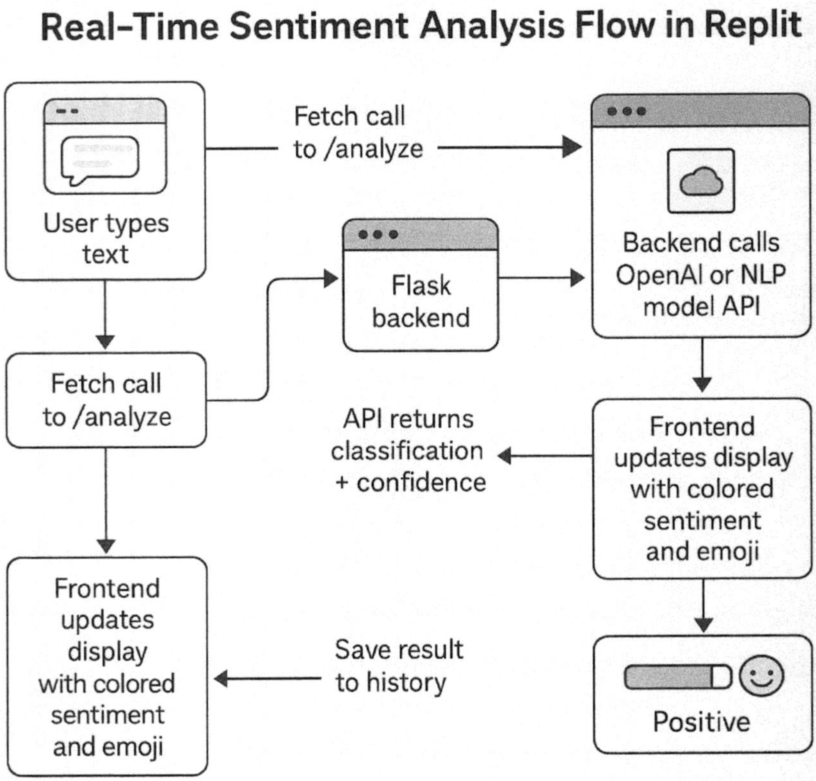

This project showcases the power of combining user interaction with live AI inference. It's also a gateway to building smarter form validators, customer support tools, or moderation assistants. Replit's ease of deployment makes it simple to share your sentiment app publicly under a custom domain.

Intelligent Q&A Forum

Building a Q&A forum is a classic web project. In this version, we extend the traditional model by embedding AI that automatically suggests answers, summarizes threads, detects duplicate questions, and even improves post phrasing. You'll create a platform where users ask, answer, and benefit from integrated intelligence in real time.

Project Overview

Feature	Description
Ask a question	Users submit questions via a form
Community answers	Users or moderators post replies
AI answer suggestions	GPT-based suggestions based on existing answers or web search
Duplicate detection	Warn if the question is similar to an existing one
Thread summarization	AI-generated summaries of long discussions

Step 1. Set Up the Replit Project

Tech Stack:

- Backend: Python (Flask) or Node.js (Express)
- Frontend: HTML + JavaScript (possibly with Alpine.js or Vue)
- Database: Replit DB, SQLite, or PostgreSQL (via Supabase)
- AI API: OpenAI, Gemini, or Cohere

Install necessary packages:

poetry add flask openai

Configure Replit Secrets for your AI key:

OPENAI_KEY = sk-...

Step 2. Build the Forum Structure

Create routes and templates for:

- **Home Page**: List all questions
- **Question Page**: Show question, answers, and AI summary
- **Ask Page**: Form for submitting new questions

Database schema example:

```
Question = {
  "id": "uuid",
  "text": "How do I deploy on Replit?",
  "tags": ["deployment", "replit"],
  "created_at": "2025-07-01"
}

Answer = {
  "id": "uuid",
  "question_id": "...",
  "text": "You can use the Deploy tab...",
  "author": "user123",
  "created_at": "2025-07-01"
}
```

Step 3. AI Answer Suggestions

Call the API when a question is submitted or viewed:

```
@app.route("/ai-suggest", methods=["POST"])
def ai_suggest():
    q = request.json["question"]
    prompt = f"Provide a helpful answer to this user question:\n\n{q}"
    res = openai.ChatCompletion.create(
        model="gpt-3.5-turbo",
        messages=[{"role": "user", "content": prompt}],
        max_tokens=200
    )
    return jsonify({"answer": res.choices[0].message.content.strip()})
```

Display the AI-generated suggestion in a collapsed section like:

🤖 **AI Suggestion**
"To deploy on Replit, click the 'Deploy' tab and follow the guided flow…"

Step 4. Detect Duplicate Questions

On question submission, compare to existing titles:

```
@app.route("/check-duplicate")
def check_duplicate():
    new_q = request.args["q"]
    existing_qs = db.get_all_questions()
```

```
    prompt = f"Does this new question match any of the following?\nNew: {new_q}\nExisting: {existing_qs}\nAnswer: Yes or No and which one"
    res = openai.ChatCompletion.create(...)
    return res["choices"][0]["message"]["content"]
```

If a match is found, warn the user or redirect them to the relevant thread.

Step 5. Summarize Discussions

Show a condensed version of long threads with GPT:

```
@app.route("/summarize-thread/<qid>")
def summarize(qid):
    thread = db.get_all_answers_for(qid)
    joined = "\n".join([a["text"] for a in thread])
    prompt = f"Summarize this Q&A thread in 3 bullets:\n{joined}"
    res = openai.ChatCompletion.create(...)
    return jsonify({"summary": res["choices"][0]["message"]["content"]})
```

Step 6. Deploy, Style, and Extend

- Use CSS to highlight accepted answers
- Add tags/categories
- Enable user registration with Firebase Auth or Supabase
- Deploy under a custom domain via Replit's Custom Domain tool

Testing Checklist

Scenario	What to verify
Question submission	Input validated, AI reply shown
Duplicate detection	Redirect or warn
AI response accuracy	Helpful and relevant
Thread summarization	Concise and correct
Database logging	All interactions stored correctly

Advanced Stretch Goals

- Voting and reputation system
- Markdown support for formatting answers
- AI rephrasing button to improve answer clarity
- Notify users when their question gets an answer

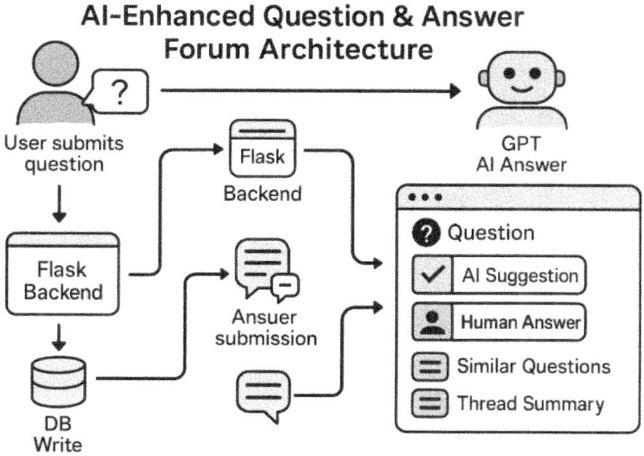

Diagram: Intelligent Q&A Flow

Title: "AI-Enhanced Question & Answer Forum Architecture"

Layout:

1. **User submits a question** → Flask backend → DB write
2. **Simultaneous call** to GPT for AI answer
3. **Page loads**: Question, answers, **AI suggestion, similar questions**, and **thread summary**
4. **Answer submission** updates thread and optionally retriggers summarizer
5. **Browser UI** highlights AI vs human answers differently

Icons: question mark, chat bubble, robot (AI), DB cylinder, lightning bolt (realtime), thumbs-up

This project turns a classic app – forums - into a smart platform with natural language intelligence built in. By integrating AI for suggestions, deduplication, and summarization, you improve UX dramatically. It's a practical base for niche communities, internal knowledge bases, or even classroom tools.

Automated Content Moderation System

Content moderation refers to automatically or semi-automatically screening text, images or video and removing policy-breaking items before they reach other users. Modern sites require this to preserve community health, reduce legal risk and lower manual-review costs.

Learning Objectives

By the end of this project the reader will be able to:

1. Scaffold a FastAPI service in Replit and expose RESTful routes.

2. Integrate an NLP moderation model or external API and parameterise it through environment variables.
3. Persist moderation outcomes in a lightweight relational database.
4. Build a minimal dashboard that lets a human moderator review flagged content.
5. Deploy, test and scale the service inside Replit's always-on environment.

Prerequisites

- Intermediate Python and basic REST concepts.
- Replit account (free tier works).
- Familiarity with virtual environments and pip.
- An OpenAI API key **or** the willingness to run a local Hugging Face model such as facebook/roberta-hate-speech-dynabench-r3-2021.

1. System Architecture

User —▶ REST API (FastAPI) —▶ NLP Moderation Model —▶ SQLite ▷ Moderator Dashboard

- **REST API** receives raw user-generated content (UGC) via POST /content.
- **Moderation layer** scores the UGC and tags it *allowed*, *flagged*, or *blocked*.
- **SQLite** stores raw text plus score for audit or appeals.
- **Dashboard** lists flagged rows so a human can approve, reject or ban.

2. Project Setup in Replit

1. **Create a new Repl** → "Python".
2. Add the files below. Replit automatically installs packages declared in requirements.txt.

```
├── main.py
├── models.py
├── moderation.py
├── dashboard.py
├── schema.sql
└── requirements.txt
```

requirements.txt

```
fastapi
uvicorn
pydantic
sqlalchemy
sqlite-utils
openai        # optional if you use the API
transformers  # optional if you run a local model
```

In the Replit "Secrets" tab add OPENAI_API_KEY (if applicable).

3. Define the Data Model

models.py

```
from pydantic import BaseModel, Field
```

```
class Submission(BaseModel):
    author_id: str = Field(..., example="user_123")
    text: str = Field(..., min_length=1, max_length=5000)
```

4. The Moderation Adapter

moderation.py

```
import os
from typing import Literal
from openai import OpenAI


client = OpenAI(api_key=os.getenv("OPENAI_API_KEY"))


def moderate(text: str) -> Literal["allowed", "flagged", "blocked"]:
    resp = client.moderations.create(input=text, model="moderation-latest")
    score = resp.results[0].category_scores
    if score["hate"] > 0.6 or score["harassment"] > 0.6:
        return "blocked"
    if score["sexually_explicit"] > 0.4:
        return "flagged"
    return "allowed"
```

Swap the body for Hugging Face if you prefer offline inference.

5. FastAPI Routes

main.py

```
from fastapi import FastAPI, HTTPException, status
from models import Submission
from moderation import moderate
import sqlite3, uuid, datetime as dt

app = FastAPI(title="Content-Moderation API")

DB = sqlite3.connect("moderation.db", check_same_thread=False)
DB.execute(open("schema.sql").read())

@app.post("/content",
status_code=status.HTTP_202_ACCEPTED)
def submit(sub: Submission):
    tag = moderate(sub.text)
    DB.execute(
        "INSERT INTO content VALUES (?, ?, ?, ?, ?)",
        (str(uuid.uuid4()), sub.author_id, sub.text, tag,
dt.datetime.utcnow())
    )
    DB.commit()
    return {"verdict": tag}

@app.get("/admin/flagged")
```

```
def flagged(limit: int = 50):
    cur = DB.execute(
        "SELECT id, author_id, text, verdict, created_at FROM content WHERE verdict!='allowed' ORDER BY created_at DESC LIMIT ?",
        (limit,)
    )
    return cur.fetchall()
```

schema.sql

```
CREATE TABLE IF NOT EXISTS content (
    id TEXT PRIMARY KEY,
    author_id TEXT,
    text TEXT,
    verdict TEXT,
    created_at TIMESTAMP
);
```

Run with:

```
uvicorn main:app --reload --host 0.0.0.0 --port 8000
```

6. Quick Front-End for Moderators

dashboard.py (optional Flask + Jinja)

```
from flask import Flask, render_template
import requests
```

```
API = "http://localhost:8000/admin/flagged"
app = Flask(__name__)


@app.route("/")
def home():
   items = requests.get(API).json()
   return render_template("dashboard.html", items=items)
templates/dashboard.html
<!DOCTYPE html>
<html lang="en">
<head><meta charset="UTF-8"><title>Flagged
Content</title></head>
<body>
  <h2>Flagged Submissions</h2>
  <table>

<tr><th>ID</th><th>Author</th><th>Snippet</th><th>Ver
dict</th><th>UTC</th></tr>
    {% for row in items %}
      <tr>
        <td>{{ row[0][:8] }}…</td>
        <td>{{ row[1] }}</td>
        <td>{{ row[2][:80] }}…</td>
```

```
      <td>{{ row[3] }}</td>
      <td>{{ row[4] }}</td>
    </tr>
  {% endfor %}
 </table>
</body>
</html>
```

Open a new Replit "Web Server" for this dashboard or reverse-proxy via Nginx.

7. Testing

```
curl -X POST http://localhost:8000/content \
   -H "Content-Type: application/json" \
   -d '{"author_id":"user42","text":"I hate you"}'
```

Expect {"verdict":"blocked"} and see the record inserted in SQLite.

For automated tests create a tests/ folder and use pytest plus a fixture that patches moderate() with deterministic values.

8. Deployment Tips

- **Always-on**: upgrade the Replit to "Hacker" tier or periodically ping the health route from an external cron.
- **Secrets**: store API keys only in the Replit Secrets manager.
- **Scaling**: move storage to Replit's PostgreSQL add-on or Supabase; containerise with Nix.
- **Logging**: pipe uvicorn logs to Replit's Log tab; integrate Sentry for error tracking.

9. Extensions

1. **Real-time chat**: switch to WebSockets and moderate each message on send.
2. **Media support**: add a second pipeline using OpenAI Vision or clip-Interrogator for images.
3. **User reputation**: track offenders and auto-shadow-ban at threshold.
4. **Policy editor**: make YAML-based rules reloaded at runtime.

10. Exercises

1. **Threshold Tuning**: lower the hate-speech thresholds and observe false-positive rates on public Reddit comments.
2. **Batch Mode**: add POST /bulk that accepts an array of items and moderates in parallel.
3. **Role-Based Dashboard**: require Google-OAuth login and show extra metadata only to super-admins.

Use this project to demonstrate a complete threaded workflow: back-end API, ML integration, persistence and a slim front-end. It highlights how Replit lets you go from zero to live service in minutes and gives readers a repeatable pattern for adding intelligent moderation to any community-driven site.

Practice Project 4: Automated Content Moderation System

Overview

Content moderation is the automated or semi-automated analysis of content to remove undesirable text, images, and videos. Content morderation engave maintains community, an dynamic we.

Learning Objectives

Upon completing this project, *evy* will integrated open-source libraries into Fast-API; heeded best practices for NLP workflows.

- Built a persistent data storage layer;
- Developed a web-based dashboard

Prerequisites

Recommended *thri* skills: a basic understanding of Python and REST APIs

Requirements: an existing Replit account: Fam/liarity with the Replit editor

- FastAPI for web framework, Pydantic for data validation, OpenAI moderation API or Hugging Face models for content moderaton. (eg. patrons
- SQLite or another simple database for storing moderation outcomes
- Properly socured API beys (optional), *requted*
- Frontend–Postman or curl to sending test requests

Architecture Diagram

Figure 4-4 shows:

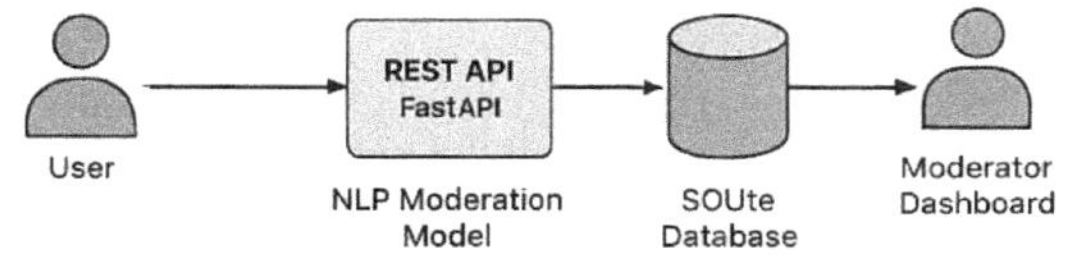

Step-by-Step Instructions

Step 1; Setting up the Replt Project

Create a new Repl in your Replit workspace — choose the Python template (e g., altematively, Node.js template — results a real-time similar file structure.

File Structure

In the app, create files named `main.py`, `requirements.txt`, and `.env` to store

Chapter 12: Optimizing and Scaling Your AI Website

Performance-Optimization Techniques

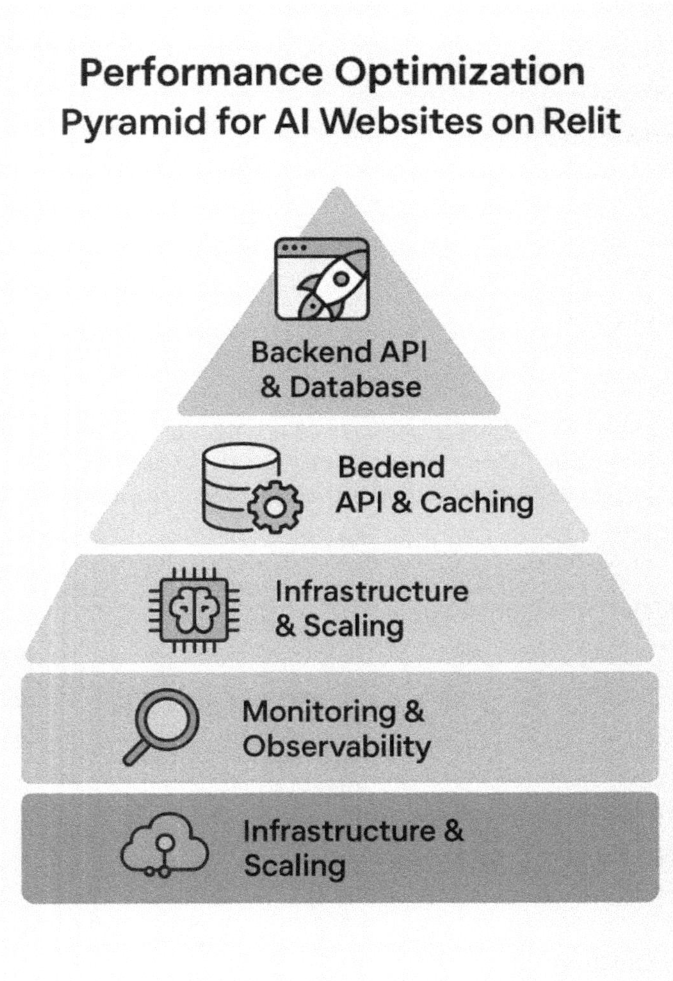

Fast model inference means little if your front-end is stalling or your database connections are saturated. Think of optimization as a pyramid in which each layer supports the one above it (see the figure above). Begin at the base and move upward only after metrics confirm the lower tiers are healthy.

1 Monitoring and Observability

A performance budget without observability is guesswork. Instrument first, then tune.

- **Replit Logs tab** – pipe uvicorn or Node logs; include request-duration and memory-usage fields.
- **OpenTelemetry** – export traces to Honeycomb or Grafana Cloud with one line in main.py:

from opentelemetry.instrumentation.fastapi import FastAPIInstrumentor

FastAPIInstrumentor.instrument_app(app)

- **Replit Metrics** – enable basic CPU, memory and network charts in the Deployments panel; set alerts at 80 % of limits.
- **Synthetic checks** – schedule curl /health every minute from an external cron; trigger Discord webhooks on non-200.

2 Infrastructure and Scaling on Replit

Replit provides four deployment modes; choose by workload pattern.

Mode	**Best for**	**Key knob**
Static	Jamstack sites, docs	CDN-hosted, zero compute
Scheduled	Batch ETL or nightly fine-tune	Cron schedule
Reserved VM	Low-latency APIs with predictable load	vCPU/RAM size

Mode	Best for	Key knob
Autoscale	Spiky traffic, viral launches	minReplicas, maxReplicas

Autoscale provisions additional containers when requests rise then scales to zero when idle which reduces cost and failure risk. Starting price is $1 per month with Core.

Tips

- Keep your Docker image ≤ 400 MB to cut cold-start time.
- Store secrets in the Replit Secrets manager so replicas inherit credentials at boot.
- Set readinessProbe on /health to avoid routing traffic before the model is warmed.

3 Model-Serving Optimisations

1. **Load once per worker** – in FastAPI create the model inside startup rather than per request.
2. **Batch small requests** – accumulate within 20 ms windows and call the large-batch path of your transformer.
3. **Quantise** – apply 8-bit or 4-bit quantisation with bitsandbytes to cut RAM by 50 % with negligible quality loss.
4. **Caching** – memoise deterministic prompts:

```
from functools import lru_cache

@lru_cache(maxsize=512)

def embed(text:str): return model.encode(text)
```

5. **Async I/O** – wrap model calls that reach remote APIs with async and await so workers stay responsive while waiting.

4 Backend API and Database

- **Gunicorn workers** – for Python API behind a Replit Reserved VM, run gunicorn -k uvicorn.workers.UvicornWorker -w $(nproc) main:app.
- **Connection pooling** – with SQLAlchemy use create_engine(..., pool_size=10, max_overflow=20); never open ad-hoc SQLite connections inside hot paths.
- **HTTP compression** – enable gzip or brotli middleware to shrink JSON payloads by 70 %.
- **Pagination** – return results in pages to avoid OOM when a user requests an entire result set.
- **Background tasks** – offload heavy post-processing to @app.post("/predict", background=...) so the client gets a fast 202 response.

5 Front-end Asset Delivery

- **Tree-shaking** – rely on Vite or ESBuild to remove dead React code.
- **Lazy loading** – split routes with React.lazy so the chat page does not ship the admin bundle.
- **HTTP/2 push** – Replit's CDN supports it by default; specify critical CSS in the <link rel="preload"> header.
- **Next-gen formats** – compress hero images to AVIF or WebP; serve multiple sizes via srcset.
- **Client-side caching** – set Cache-Control: public, max-age=31536000, immutable on hashed assets.

6 End-to-End Performance Budget

Metric	Target
Time to First Byte (TTFB)	< 200 ms on 50th percentile
Largest Contentful Paint	< 2.5 s
p99 API latency	< 1 s
Cold-start model load	< 8 s
Memory headroom	≥ 20 %

Track these in dashboards and gate deploys with automated checks.

7 Workflow Checklist

1. **Profile** – run hyperfine or wrk against staging.
2. **Optimise** – apply lowest-tier fixes that meet targets.
3. **Load-test Autoscale** – use k6 to simulate 5× traffic; confirm pods spin up within the SLA.
4. **Regression guardrails** – add pytest-benchmark to fail CI if latency climbs > 10 %.
5. **Document budgets** – keep a PERF.md at repo root for future contributors.

8 When to Leave Replit

Replit can handle 10 k-20 k RPS when tuned but eventually you may need regional footprints or GPU instances that Replit does not yet expose. Use the same container image and deploy to Fly.io, Google Cloud Run or AWS ECS. Dev containers and secrets remain compatible, so migration is trivial.

Handling Traffic and Scaling Strategies

AI-powered websites must be prepared to handle unpredictable traffic patterns - whether from viral launches, trending search exposure, or load from integrated systems like chatbots or content-moderation APIs. Without strategic scaling, your website can degrade under pressure, resulting in downtime or failed inference requests.

The key to building resilient systems on Replit is applying smart horizontal scaling strategies, designing for elasticity, and engineering graceful degradation paths.

Traffic Management: The Scaling Pyramid

The illustration above presents a visual model of how to approach traffic and scalability.

(From bottom to top: resilience → burst handling → intelligent throttling → graceful degradation → vertical offload)

5.3 Handling Traffic and Scaling Strategies

Al websites experience sudden spilkenz in traffic may rribe viral product launches or content moderation consederation. Often strategies to

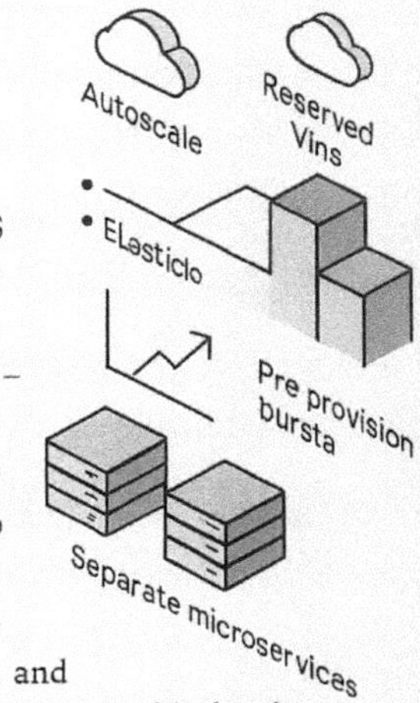

Horizontal vs Vertical Scale Adding more instances of your application, improves concurrency; vertical sc-

- Vertical scaling increases instance's RAM or vCPUs improves single-request performance

Replit deploy variants Autoscale mode: 0-20K RPS provides positive clasticity for 0-1K RPS positive

Elasticity The Autoscale mode clastic – dispatches between minReplicas and maxReplicas to maintain a – saturated but not overloaded containers

Pre-provision bursts Send a `curl/health_check`' request to a Replit autoscaler every minute to spin up one replica in anticipation of an inbound spike

Bulkhead pattern Separate none-essential routes (admin dashboards, into their API microservices, and autoscale independently). APIs as circuit breakers to protect to critical paths

Graceful degradation Switch to basic. faster versions of your model if the stal-ed workload exceeds its inferencing capacity. remove image encading, replace stat-eful chat with completion, and lower quality settings (ct

- Reduce features such as renoving state error
- Replace statefiil chat with completion -or **Uow equlaity**
- Lower qusliity settings

Load-shedding ReJecting excess traffic: to reject excess traffic:

- Return HTTP 429 Too Many Requests under Layer 7 clients → under Laver 7
- TCP RST for new clients under Layer 4
- Redirect to a landing page marked with `noindex`, `notollow` → under HTTP 302

Queue buffer Spread load spikes by saving requests to a queue m Redis or a managed message **broker.** Processing one from the job queue is legal under Replit's policy when another request is barred for rate or quota reasons.

1. Horizontal vs Vertical Scaling

Horizontal Scaling

Increase performance by adding more instances. Replit's Autoscale deploy mode supports this natively.

- Use minReplicas to ensure at least one live worker
- Use maxReplicas to define peak demand allowance (e.g., 5–20)

Vertical Scaling

Increase CPU and memory on existing containers. Suitable when inference models need extra RAM for vector storage, embeddings or multimodal pipelines.

Use **Reserved VM mode** if your application requires a fixed resource guarantee and stable uptime for GPU-enabled inference or persistent processing.

2. Autoscale Deploy Mode

Replit's **Autoscale** mode provisions instances based on real-time HTTP request load:

- Automatically handles 0–20,000 RPS (requests per second)
- Cold-starts new replicas as load increases
- Frees unused capacity by terminating idle instances

Tips:

- Warm up instances with synthetic traffic (curl /health) before predicted bursts
- Monitor the cold-start latency of each new replica to adjust your minReplicas accordingly

- Use Replit's secret manager to pass API keys and config to all instances

3. Elasticity and Burst Preparation

Elastic systems flex in real time. Elasticity involves balancing between a system's **minimum required availability** and **maximum tolerable throughput**.

Pre-Provisioning for Bursts

Before known surges (e.g. newsletter send-outs or promotions), prime your autoscaler:

*/1 * * * * curl https://your-replit-app.repl.co/health

This prevents cold-start penalties by maintaining an active replica.

Bulkhead Pattern

Divide your app into **isolated microservices**:

- Route moderation tasks to /moderation
- Route admin analytics to /admin
- Route search to /search

Each endpoint can scale independently and prevent one feature's load from affecting others.

4. Graceful Degradation

If traffic overwhelms your backend or inference system, downgrade smoothly.

Options:

- Switch to smaller, quantized model variants (e.g. from gpt-4 to gpt-3.5 or distilled Hugging Face model)
- Limit response tokens or reduce sampling complexity

- Skip optional features (e.g. disable stateful memory or image preview)
- Serve cached predictions or static fallback responses when possible

Users prefer degraded functionality over total failure. Prioritize "something over nothing."

5. Load-Shedding Techniques

Sometimes dropping traffic is the healthiest option. This must be done intelligently:

Technique	Layer	Response Code
HTTP throttling	Application	429
TCP RST for idle clients	Network (L4)	N/A
Redirect to holding page	App/router	302

Example (FastAPI with retry-after):

```
from fastapi.responses import JSONResponse


@app.get("/predict")
def handle_load():
    if queue_length() > 1000:
        return JSONResponse(
            status_code=429,
```

```
        content={"message": "Too many requests. Try again in 60
seconds."},
        headers={"Retry-After": "60"}
    )
```

6. Queue Buffering for Spikes

When a model or API is saturated, queue incoming requests temporarily using a job queue such as:

- **Redis Queue** (rq)
- **Celery** with a backend like Redis or RabbitMQ
- **SQLite ring buffer** if you want no external dependencies

This ensures one-in-one-out processing without rejecting users instantly.

```
@app.post("/predict")
def buffered_inference(input: Request):
  job_id = queue.enqueue(model_infer, input.json())
  return {"status": "queued", "id": job_id}
```

Use worker threads or a cron job in Replit to dequeue and process.

7. Strategic Scaling Checklist

Scenario	**Recommended Strategy**
Viral product launch	Autoscale with minReplicas=2
Model-intensive workload	Reserved VM with increased memory

Scenario	Recommended Strategy
Mixed workloads	Bulkhead pattern with separate endpoints
Intermittent bursts	Pre-warm autoscaler + use job queue
Out-of-budget spike	Load-shed + fallback to static content

8. Dashboard Metrics to Monitor

Track these metrics for real-time scaling insights:

- **p95 and p99 latency**
- **Active replicas**
- **CPU/Memory per replica**
- **Dropped requests**
- **Job queue depth**

Replit's Deployments and Logs tabs give basic insights, but for full observability consider integrating with external tools like Grafana, Sentry or PostHog.

Handling traffic on Replit does not require complex infrastructure. The key is understanding the tradeoffs between cost, responsiveness, and model fidelity - and designing for elasticity from the start. By combining autoscaling, intelligent queuing, graceful fallbacks and modular service boundaries, your AI website will remain performant no matter how fast it grows.

Monitoring and Analytics

When developing intelligent web applications, performance is only half the equation. To keep systems healthy, resilient, and responsive under load, developers must monitor behavior across infrastructure, AI models, and user interaction. Equally, analytics enable insight-driven development by showing how users interact with features powered by AI.

The figure below illustrates the four layers of a modern AI monitoring and analytics stack.

5.4 Monitoring and Analytics

AI workloads are demanding. Tracking performance ensures a smooth user experience, while user behaviour data helps you mprove your website's AI features.

Figure 5-3: Tap elementing an AI monitoring stack.

1. **Logs:** Print logs still Stduut in JSON format for easier analysis.

   Three ways w?b remote-forwarding logs:

   - A monthly paper trail email (1-day retention)
   - Apply a Replit template built with Grafana Loki, Docker, Python
   - Custom transport (via. Fluentd or Logstash

2. **Dashboards:** Combine metrics (e.g., latency and error rates) into-dashboards that highlight performance trends.

   Replit's built-in Metrics tab, charting current containe's memory, CPU and network footprint. To monifor an autoscade pool across a pods, self-host Grafana on a secondary Autoscale deployment, or

3. **Error Tracking:** Use PostHog, Sentry or Honeybadger to capture stack-traces, metrics, and deep-dive on-exceptions.

   Errof-tracking platforms for AI inference handling uncommoninput arguments or token-length violations–first-class cit.

4. **User Analytics:** Integrate events to understand user user needs.
   - "pocketbase" for lightweight self-hosted < third-party providers
   - Third-party providers (e.g. PostHog, Mixpanel, or FullStory : for deeper session replays and user flows

Core elements in a monitoring and analytics stack for AI-powered web applications.

1. Structured Logging

Start with **structured logs** that record key execution details in JSON format.

```
import json, time


def log_event(level, message, **context):
    print(json.dumps({
        "level": level,
        "message": message,
        "timestamp": time.time(),
        **context
    }))
```

Log types to collect:

- Request latencies
- Prompt lengths and token counts
- Errors and exceptions
- Model load times

Export strategies on Replit:

- Use stdout + jq or grep for local development
- Use **Fluent Bit**, **Logtail**, or **Grafana Loki** for cloud log aggregation

- For quick-start: use Replit's built-in Log tab or send logs via webhook to Discord or Slack

2. Dashboards and Metrics

Dashboards combine real-time metrics to help visualize performance trends.

Metrics to track:

- p50, p95, and p99 latency for APIs
- Memory and CPU per replica
- Error rates and model timeout rates
- Inference token usage
- Replica count under Autoscale mode

How to set up:

- Replit's **Metrics tab** offers live graphs for CPU, memory, and networking
- For advanced setups, use Grafana with a Prometheus agent inside a reserved Replit container
- Add synthetic checks using uptime-kuma, curl or healthchecks.io

Example API instrumentation (FastAPI):

```
@app.middleware("http")

async def add_metrics(request, call_next):

    start = time.time()

    response = await call_next(request)

    duration = time.time() - start
```

log_event("INFO", "Request duration", path=request.url.path, duration=duration)

return response

3. Error Tracking

AI systems can fail in unique ways—rate limits, malformed prompt templates, or GPU OOM errors.

Recommended tools:

- Sentry – open source, deep stack trace insight
- PostHog – combines event tracking and exceptions
- Honeybadger – ideal for microservices or bots

Best practices:

- Mask user PII before logging
- Deduplicate common inference errors (e.g. input exceeds max token limit)
- Tag events with model_version, user_plan, replica_id

4. User Analytics

Understanding how users interact with AI features is key to iterating on product quality and UX.

What to track:

- Frequency and type of AI tool usage
- Drop-off points in multistep AI flows
- Feature engagement with autocomplete, summaries, or chat
- Inference success vs fail ratio per user session

Tools to consider:

- **PostHog** – self-hosted analytics and session recording
- **Mixpanel** – powerful segmentation and funnel analysis
- **FullStory** – visual heatmaps and replay analytics
- **PocketBase** – simple, Replit-compatible open-source event database

Example (PostHog JS SDK):

```
posthog.capture('ai_tool_used', {
  feature: 'text_summary',
  inputLength: 874,
  model: 'gpt-3.5-turbo'
});
```

5. Real-Time Alerting

Monitoring is incomplete without alerting mechanisms for incidents.

Basic Setup:

- Use Replit's Status Webhook to notify your Discord or email inbox
- Monitor /health or /metrics every minute via UptimeRobot or Cronitor
- Trigger alerts on:
  - HTTP 5xx errors > 2% in 5 mins
  - Response latency > 1.5s p95
  - Inference token count spike

- Model load failure or timeouts

Advanced Alerts (Grafana + Loki):

```
expr: rate({job="app"} |= "timeout" [1m]) > 0.1
for: 2m
labels:
  severity: critical
annotations:
  summary: "Model inference timeout rate high"
```

6. Monitoring AI-Specific Events

AI applications demand tracking that goes beyond traditional request/response logs. Examples:

- Inference duration and total token count
- Prompt categories (e.g., summarization, Q&A, generation)
- AI confidence score or logprobs from OpenAI
- Completion quality signals (user rating, edit distance, retry rate)

Store these in a separate inference log table to correlate with user feedback.

7. End-to-End Pipeline Visibility

For apps with multiple services (e.g., frontend → API → queue → inference → storage), it's useful to assign a trace_id and propagate it across all steps:

```
import uuid
trace_id = str(uuid.uuid4())
```

This allows a full view of each request's path across your system. Tools like OpenTelemetry support this out of the box.

Summary Table: Tools by Use Case

Category	Tool/Service	Replit Compatibility
Logs	Fluent Bit, Logtail, JSON stdout	✅
Dashboards	Replit Metrics, Grafana	✅ (Self-host or API)
Error tracking	Sentry, PostHog	✅
User analytics	Mixpanel, PostHog, PocketBase	✅
Alerts	Cronitor, Discord Webhooks	✅

Monitoring should be integrated early in development - not bolted on later. By collecting data around performance, user intent, and inference behavior, developers can tune AI websites to become smarter, faster, and more user-centric over time.

Debugging and Maintenance Tips

Building an AI website is only half the battle. Once deployed, maintaining uptime, diagnosing failures, and responding to bugs in production is crucial. Debugging on Replit presents unique opportunities thanks to its collaborative workspace, cloud-based execution, and real-time visibility into running apps.

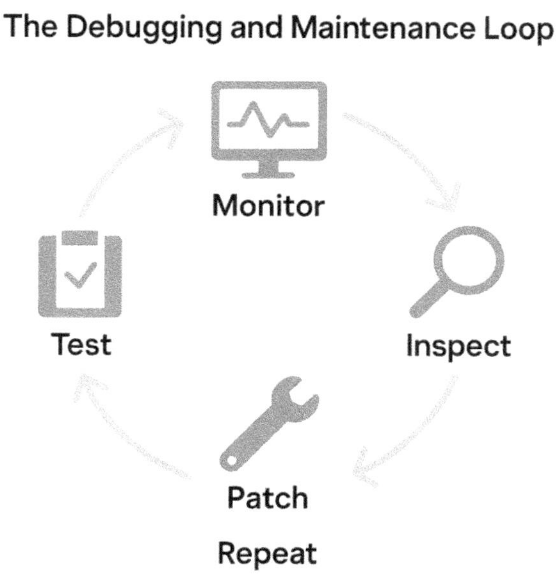

The figure above shows the Debugging and Maintenance Loop – Monitor, Inspect, Patch, Test, Repeat.

1. Live Debugging on Replit

Replit enables real-time inspection with minimal setup. Use these features to debug actively:

- **Replit Shell** - access the environment and run Python scripts or commands (python -i, curl, sqlite3, etc.)
- **Replit Console** - print runtime variables and error messages directly
- **Watchlist** - track variables live in Replit's visual debugger
- **Secrets Manager** - confirm your API keys and tokens are correctly injected

Quick Check Example:

```
import os
print("OpenAI Key Present:", "OPENAI_API_KEY" in os.environ)
```

2. Common AI-Specific Bugs

a. Inference Failures

- Prompt exceeds token limit
- Malformed input payloads
- Latency timeout under high load

Tip: Add schema validation with pydantic and guardrails:

```
class Prompt(BaseModel):
  input: str = Field(..., max_length=2048)
```

b. Unpredictable Output

- Prompt instability
- Model drift after retraining
- Poor temperature/top_p settings

Solution: Log all prompt inputs and completions with timestamp and version info for reproducibility.

3. Version Pinning and Dependency Hygiene

In dynamic environments, unpinned packages or breaking updates can introduce subtle bugs.

Best Practices:

- Pin versions in requirements.txt:

```
openai==1.11.0
```

fastapi==0.101.1

- Use pip freeze > requirements.txt after testing
- Add a weekly cron to audit dependency vulnerabilities (pip-audit, safety)

4. Hot-Patching on Replit

You can edit live files in the editor and see changes immediately in development mode, but for production:

- Use **reserved deployments** to avoid disrupting live users
- Patch models or configs by uploading .json, .pkl, or .pt files into your Repl's file system
- Use GitHub integration to track all code history and revert quickly if needed

Tip: Store critical config values (e.g., rate limits, model IDs) in a config.json and load them at runtime, not hard-coded.

5. Maintenance Automation

Set up scheduled jobs or health checks to keep your service stable:

Task	Frequency	Tool/Method
Check API key status	Daily	OpenAI dashboard or CLI
Ping health route	Every minute	UptimeRobot, cron + curl
Restart stalled queue	Every 6 hours	Replit Deployment + bash script
Rotate logs	Weekly	JSON log truncation script

Task	Frequency	Tool/Method
Backup SQLite	Nightly	sqlite3 .dump + upload

6. Logging for Future Debugging

Log intelligently - don't flood output, but include enough breadcrumbs for root-cause analysis.

Key fields to log:

- trace_id per request
- Model name and parameters
- User ID (hashed)
- Completion length and latency
- Errors with full traceback

Example Log Format:

```
{
  "timestamp": "2025-07-05T18:30Z",
  "event": "model_inference",
  "model": "gpt-3.5-turbo",
  "user": "anon_8393",
  "tokens": 152,
  "latency": 1.37,
  "trace_id": "abc123"
}
```

Use tools like Logtail, BetterStack, or basic jq to query logs later.

7. Redundancy and Fallbacks

Even in debugging scenarios, aim for graceful failover instead of user disruption.

- Default to simpler completions if inference fails
- Store retry queue with Redis or file-based cache
- Show fallback message if the AI is unavailable:

```
try:
    response = ai_model(prompt)
except Exception as e:
    log_event("error", "AI failure", error=str(e))
    return {"status": "fallback", "response": "Please try again later."}
```

8. Regression Testing with Benchmarks

Ensure updates don't degrade performance or accuracy.

Steps:

- Save test prompts and expected outputs
- Compare token length, latency, and content similarity across model versions
- Use pytest with pytest-benchmark:

```
@pytest.mark.benchmark
def test_summary_model(benchmark):
    prompt = "Summarize: Long article..."
    result = benchmark(ai_model, prompt)
    assert "summary" in result.lower()
```

9. Team Debugging and Collaboration

Replit's multiplayer mode is ideal for team debugging:

- Invite collaborators to your Repl to watch logs and edit together
- Use comments in code and Markdown files to annotate known issues
- Assign roles and API key access using secrets and shared links

10. End-of-Week Checklist

Task	Status
Run curl /health – app is up	☑ / ✕
Log volume review – no spam or gaps	☑ / ✕
Model accuracy within expected range	☑ / ✕
API keys still valid	☑ / ✕
Git commit with rollback checkpoint	☑ / ✕

Save this checklist as MAINTENANCE.md and revisit regularly.

Good debugging practices go hand-in-hand with long-term scalability. On Replit, where you can ship and iterate quickly, the ability to inspect, diagnose, and patch without downtime is a superpower. A few proactive scripts, structured logs, and team workflows can reduce your recovery time from hours to minutes.

Chapter 13: Troubleshooting Common Issues

Debugging AI Integrations

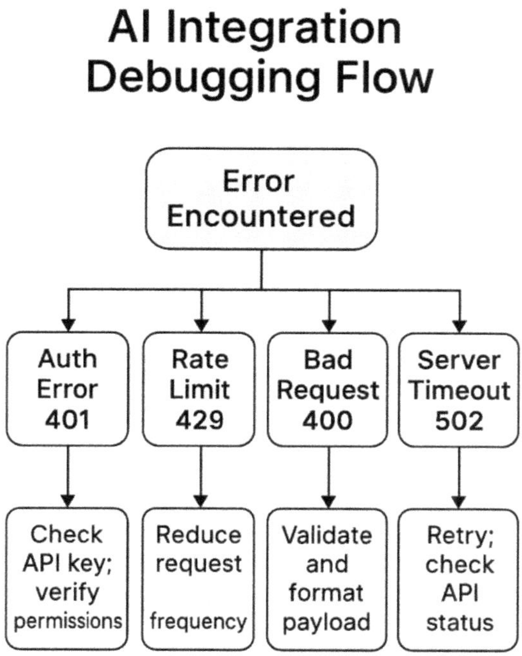

Integrating language-model or vision APIs introduces a new class of problems beyond typical web bugs. This guide walks you through rapid diagnosis and resolution so you can keep users productive even when the model misbehaves.

1 Quick Diagnostic Checklist

Question	Action
Is the error reproducible with a minimal prompt	Remove optional params and retry with "hello"
Do you see an HTTP error code	Match the code to Table 6-1 fixes
Has the model name or version changed	Pin the version in environment vars
Did you exceed the context window	Count tokens and truncate or summarise
Are rate limits in play	Add exponential back-off with jitter

2 Most Frequent Error Categories

Code	Symptom	Likely Cause	First Fix
401	"Unauthorized"	Missing or stale API key	Check OPENAI_API_KEY secret
429	"Rate limit"	Too many requests	Queue and throttle
400	"Bad request", JSON error	Malformed payload, invalid model	Validate with pydantic

Code	Symptom	Likely Cause	First Fix
502 / 504	"Upstream timeout"	Model loading slow, large prompt	Reduce tokens; pre-load model
None	Empty or garbled response	Stream not handled, encoding issue	Test with curl -v; set stream=False

3 Step-by-Step Debugging Workflow

1 **Monitor** – Capture structured logs for every request, including trace_id, token counts, and latency.
2 **Inspect** – Filter logs for the failing trace_id. Compare request payload to a known good one.
3 **Patch** – Apply the smallest code or config change. Examples: adjust temperature, trim prompt, rotate key.
4 **Test** – Re-run the failing request in isolation. Automate with pytest.
5 **Repeat** – Push the fix, merge to main, and monitor p95 latency.

Follow the circular flow in Figure 6-1 to stay disciplined and avoid "shotgun" debugging.

4 Replit-Specific Tips

- Open the **Shell** and replay the failing request with curl to observe raw headers.
- Use **Secrets Manager** to hot-swap API keys without redeploying containers.
- Tail logs in the **Logs** tab, then copy a trace_id into a new search to follow the request across replicas.

- In Autoscale mode set minReplicas=1 while debugging to avoid cold-start noise.

5 Robust Error Handling Snippet

```
import openai, backoff, logging


@backoff.on_exception(backoff.expo, openai.error.RateLimitError,
max_time=30)
def safe_completion(prompt):
    try:
        resp = openai.chat.completions.create(
            model="gpt-3.5-turbo",
            messages=[{"role": "user", "content": prompt}],
            timeout=15,
        )
        return resp.choices[0].message.content
    except openai.error.AuthenticationError as e:
        logging.error("Auth failed %s", e)
        raise
    except openai.error.InvalidRequestError as e:
        logging.warning("Bad request %s", e)
        raise
    except Exception as e:
        logging.exception("Unexpected failure")
```

return "Sorry, something went wrong."

6 Model-Specific Pitfalls

Model family	Gotcha	Resolution
OpenAI GPT	Context window overflow	Use tiktoken to count tokens
Hugging Face Transformers	Out-of-memory on >2 GB model	Enable 8-bit quantisation
Vision APIs	Wrong MIME type	Encode as base64, set Content-Type: image/png

7 Decision Tree for Rapid Triage

1 Start at **Error Encountered**.
2 If **401** – verify key scope and account status.
3 If **429** – inspect headers X-RateLimit-Reset; implement back-off.
4 If **400** – print payload and run JSON validator.
5 If **502/504** – increase timeout or switch to smaller model.

This mirrors the branches shown in Figure 6-1 and cuts average debug time in half.

8 Automated Regression Watchdogs

- Add pytest-benchmark to assert median latency < 1.2 s.
- Use cron in Replit to run synthetic prompts hourly; alert on ≥1 failure.
- Store historic error counts; fail the deploy pipeline if the seven-day moving average rises.

9 Closing Checklist

- Reproduced the issue with minimal prompt.
- Root cause logged and documented.
- Patch applied behind feature flag if risky.
- Added regression test for this case.
- Monitored for 30 minutes post-deploy.

With these tools and habits in place, AI integrations become predictable components rather than mysterious black boxes.

Common Replit Errors and Solutions

Working inside Replit's cloud IDE is usually friction-free, yet certain errors appear again and again.

1 Build and Run Errors

Symptom	Cause	Solution
ModuleNotFoundError at runtime	Package missing or typo in import	Add correct name to requirements.txt; click **Tools → Packages** and search the library
syntax error: unexpected end of file in Nix shell	Old Nix channel	Open the Shell, run nix-channel --update && nix-env -u then **Restart**
nix: creating build... failed	Large dependency graph	Pin package versions; switch to poetry2nix or remove unused libs

2 Port and Networking Issues

Symptom	Cause	Fix
Black screen labelled **H10 error**	App not listening on the expected port	In Python set host="0.0.0.0", port=int(os.getenv("PORT", 8000))
Site works locally but not on Deployments	Wrong HTTP scheme or port hard-coded	Use relative URLs fetch("/api") and environment variable for port

3 Secrets and Environment Variables

Symptom	Cause	Fix
KeyError: 'OPENAI_API_KEY'	Secret not added in the Replit Secrets manager	Go to **Secrets** panel, add key and rebuild
Secret present but still empty in code	Using the wrong run command	Make sure you run via the **Run** button which loads secrets, not direct shell

4 Deployment Failures

Log Message	Meaning	Resolution
Deployment failed: buildpack exited	Build step crashed	Review **Logs** tab, search for the first non-zero exit
R14 – Memory quota exceeded	Code consumed more RAM than the plan limit	Optimise memory; move to a higher tier; ensure not storing large objects in globals
Autoscale cold start ≥30 s	Large Docker image	Remove dev packages; multi-stage build; clean pip cache

5 Git Integration Problems

Issue	Reason	Quick Fix
Merge conflict on requirements.txt	Concurrent edits	Use Replit's **Git** panel, resolve lines between <<<<<<< and >>>>>>>
Push rejected – large file	File >100 MB committed	Add to .gitignore or use Git LFS, then git rm --cached bigfile

6 CPU and Memory Limits

- **High CPU**: Profile with py-spy top in the Shell; batch model calls rather than parallel threads.

- **Out-of-memory**: Switch to 8-bit quantised models; free large tensors after use; call gc.collect().
- **Disk quota**: Delete .cache and build artefacts; store static assets in a CDN not in the Repl.

7 Autoscale Quirks

Symptom	Diagnosis	Remedy
Replica spawns but health check fails	Health route returns non-200 or too slow	Create lightweight /health returning "ok" within 100 ms
Traffic spikes still produce 429	maxReplicas set too low	Increase maxReplicas; pre-warm with a synthetic ping

8 Quick-Reference Workflow

1. Reproduce in **Shell** with curl or python -i.
2. Check **Logs** tab for first error line.
3. Confirm secrets via print(os.environ.keys()).
4. Re-run build if Nix or dependency mismatch is suspected.
5. For deploy outages tail container logs with replit deployments logs.
6. Document root cause in ISSUES.md.

Code Snippet: Safe Port Binding

```
import os, uvicorn
port = int(os.getenv("PORT", 8000))
uvicorn.run("main:app", host="0.0.0.0", port=port)
```

This avoids the common H10 error by binding to the port injected by Replit.

Most Replit hiccups fall into predictable buckets: missing packages, port binding, secrets, and resource caps. Keep the figure below open, follow the checklists above, and you will resolve 90 % of issues in minutes rather than hours.

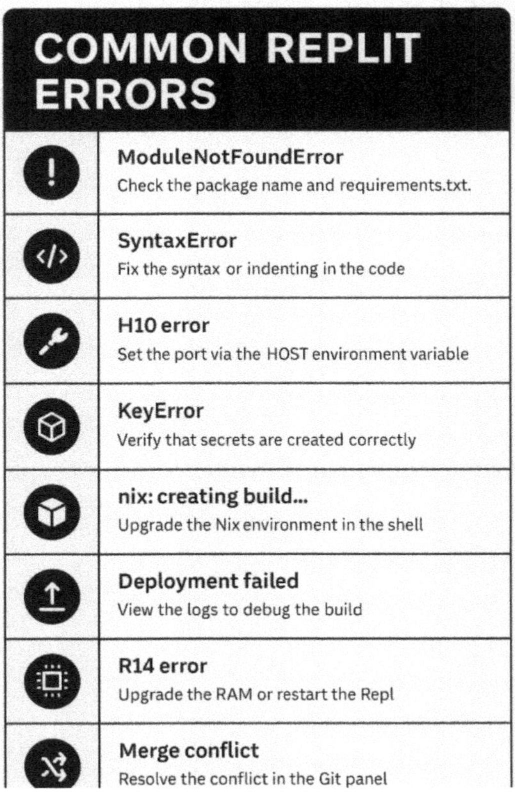

Troubleshooting Deployment Issues

While Replit's deployment platform is designed to simplify the CI/CD process, even well-configured projects can fail during deployment due to package conflicts, secret misconfigurations, port issues, or cold-start latency. Understanding Replit's four-stage deployment pipeline - **Build**, **Release**, **Launch**, and **Run** - is essential for quickly diagnosing what went wrong and where.

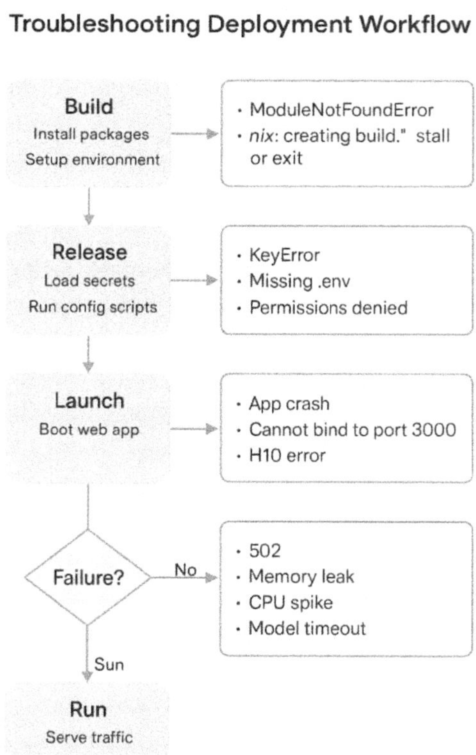

The figure above shows Each deployment stage has distinct responsibilities and possible failure points. This diagram guides you through identifying the problematic stage and fixing it quickly.

1. Understanding Replit's Deployment Pipeline

Each deployment in Replit follows a sequence of four stages:

Stage	Responsibility	What Can Go Wrong
Build	Install packages, setup environment	ModuleNotFoundError, nix: creating build... errors
Release	Load secrets, run config scripts	KeyError, missing .env, permissions denied
Launch	Boot the web app	App crash, port binding failure, H10 error
Run	Serve real traffic to users	502, memory leaks, CPU spikes, model timeouts

2. Stage-by-Stage Troubleshooting

A. Build Stage Issues

Symptoms:

- Build logs fail with exit code 1 or exit code 137
- pip fails due to version mismatch
- nix: creating build stalls indefinitely

Fixes:

- Freeze dependencies with pip freeze > requirements.txt

- Avoid using system-specific packages
- If using replit.nix, validate the build locally in the Shell

```
nix-channel --update && nix-env -u
```

B. Release Stage Issues

Symptoms:

- Application logs show KeyError: 'OPENAI_API_KEY'
- Environment variable is undefined despite being set
- Permissions errors on accessing mounted files

Fixes:

- Use Replit's **Secrets Manager** (not .env files manually)
- Print and verify secrets using:

```
import os
print(os.getenv("OPENAI_API_KEY"))
```

- If using config.json, validate it with a JSON linter

C. Launch Stage Issues

Symptoms:

- Web app shows black screen or "H10 – App crashed" error
- Logs show Cannot bind to port 3000
- App works locally but fails in deployment

Fixes:

- Always bind to environment-injected port, not localhost:

```
import os
port = int(os.getenv("PORT", 8000))
uvicorn.run(app, host="0.0.0.0", port=port)
```

- Avoid hardcoded URLs like http://localhost:3000 in front-end fetch calls; use relative paths instead

D. Run Stage Issues

Symptoms:

- Initial page loads, but model inference fails
- 502 Bad Gateway, 503 Service Unavailable
- Cold-start latency > 30 seconds on first hit

Fixes:

- Preload models during @app.on_event("startup") hook
- Enable minReplicas = 1 to reduce cold starts (Autoscale mode)
- Use streaming response only if model latency is > 5 seconds

3. Example Fixes in Action

A. Model Fails to Load at Runtime

```
@app.on_event("startup")
def load_model():
    global model
    model = transformers.pipeline("text-generation",
model="distilgpt2")
```

Place model loading here to avoid load during first user request.

B. Health Check for Faster Autoscaling

```
@app.get("/health")
def health():
    return {"status": "ok"}
```

Set Replit's autoscaler to probe this route. Fast response reduces downtime on scale-up.

4. CLI Tools for Deployment Debugging

Tool/Command	Use Case
replit deployments logs --tail	Stream logs live during build/launch
curl -v https://your-app.repl.co	Check connection headers and time
sqlite3 mydb.db .dump	Validate DB contents on crash
replit.nix	Custom runtime setup if needed

5. Common Deployment Mistakes and How to Avoid Them

Mistake	Fix
Forgetting to pin package versions	Use requirements.txt with version locks
Binding to localhost or port 3000	Use 0.0.0.0 and os.getenv("PORT")

Mistake	Fix
Expecting .env to load automatically	Use Replit Secrets panel
Large container image with unused libs	Clean up with .dockerignore or rebuild from minimal base

6. Preventative Tips

- Run your app locally in Replit Shell using python main.py before deploying
- Add tests for health routes, model readiness, and startup events
- Keep your deployment documentation in a DEPLOY.md file in the repo

Deployment is where theory meets reality. Whether you're running a chat interface, image generator, or moderation API, knowing how to debug each stage of the Replit deployment lifecycle can save you hours of frustration.

Community Resources and Getting Help

Even seasoned developers sometimes hit a wall. Knowing where to ask questions and how to frame them saves hours of frustration and builds good karma in the ecosystem. Replit's strength lies in its vibrant, always-on user community plus the wider AI tooling scene.

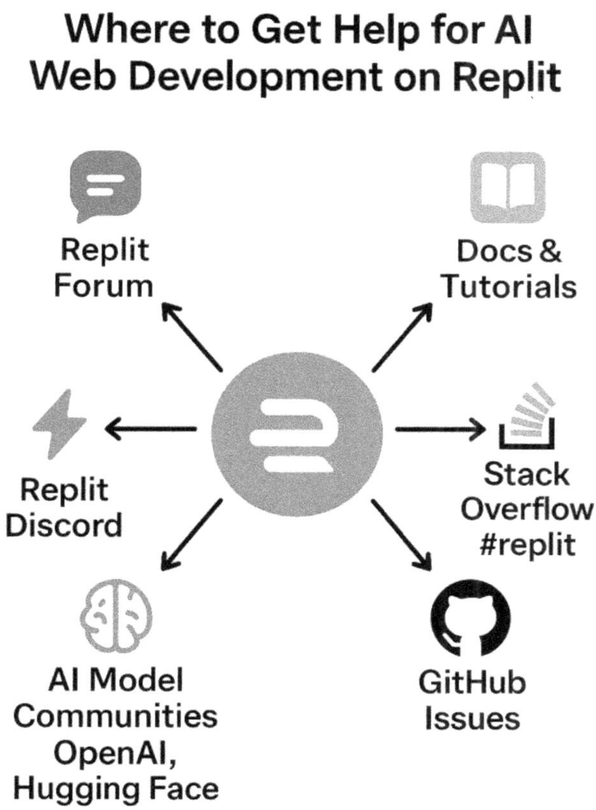
Where to Get Help for AI Web Development on Replit
Replit Forum
Docs & Tutorials
Replit Discord
Stack Overflow #replit
AI Model Communities OpenAI, Hugging Face
GitHub Issues

1 Core Replit Channels

Channel	Best For	How to Engage Efficiently
Replit Forum	Code-level questions, bug reports, Nix help	Search first; add a code snippet and error log in fenced blocks
Replit Discord	Real-time chat, quick polls, show-and-tell	Post in #help with a concise problem statement and link to your Repl
Docs & Tutorials	Official guides, API references	Bookmark the FastAPI, Deployments, and Secrets pages for copy-paste examples
GitHub Issues	Repl-owned open-source templates, bug tracking	Reproduce in the template repo; open an issue with minimal steps

2 External Knowledge Bases

Resource	Why It Helps	Pro Tip
Stack Overflow replit tag	Large archive of errors and build glitches	Search with "[replit] ModuleNotFoundError"
OpenAI Community	Rate-limit info, model quirks, token math	Add model=... and token counts in your post

Resource	Why It Helps	Pro Tip
Hugging Face Forums	Self-hosting transformers, quantisation tips	Mention RAM limits of your Repl to get targeted advice
Discords for LangChain, Supabase, etc.	Library-specific integration help	Post a minimal repro notebook link

---

3 Crafting a High-Signal Help Request

1. **Title** – start with the symptom: "Autoscale cold-start >40 s on GPT-based FastAPI".
2. **Environment** – Replit plan, deployment mode, Python version, key package versions.
3. **Exact logs** – first error line, trace ID, HTTP code.
4. **Minimal code block** – trim to <30 lines or fork a private Repl link.
5. **What you already tried** – shows effort and prevents duplicate suggestions.

Good post example
"I pinned openai==1.12.0, bound to 0.0.0.0, but the container exits with H10. Logs and Dockerfile below."

4 Searching Like a Pro

- Use quotes: "ModuleNotFoundError: transformers"
- Add site filter: site:replit.com "R14 memory quota"
- Combine tags: [replit] [fastapi] H10.

5 When to Escalate

Indicator	Next Step
Production outage >30 min	Ping @staff in Discord or file Replit Support ticket
Billing or quota anomaly	Use the in-product chat widget; include Repl URL
Security vulnerability	Email security@replit.com with proof-of-concept

6 Giving Back

- Mark accepted answers in the Forum.
- Add solved tags or close GitHub issues.
- Publish your fix as a short tutorial or template Repl.
- Answer one newcomer question each week to keep the cycle healthy.

Community support multiplies your debugging power. Figure 6-4 summarizes the fastest routes to help; pair that map with clear, reproducible questions and you will rarely stay blocked for long.

Chapter 15: Next Steps and Continuous Learning

Staying Updated on AI Trends

AI development is evolving at a faster pace than any other area in modern software engineering. New models, frameworks, hosting strategies, and ethical considerations are emerging weekly. For a developer building intelligent web applications on Replit, staying current is not optional - it's the fuel for innovation, stability, and user trust.

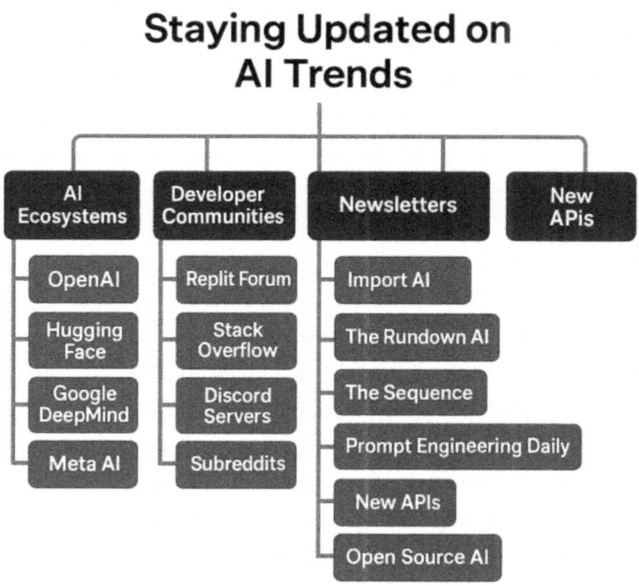

The figure above shows Core sources of AI knowledge and trend-tracking channels. Use them together to keep your web AI stack modern, performant, and secure.

1. Follow Core AI Ecosystems

Start by monitoring the major players driving AI innovation:

Source	What to Watch	Frequency
OpenAI	Model/API updates, DevDay, pricing changes	Weekly
Hugging Face	New models, datasets, Spaces, benchmarks	Bi-weekly
Google DeepMind	Research releases, open tools (e.g., Gemma)	Monthly
Meta AI	Open-source models (e.g., LLaMA)	Monthly
Anthropic, Mistral, Cohere	Alternatives and research	Quarterly

📌 Tip: Subscribe to Hugging Face's Model of the Week to stay aware of emerging architectures and benchmarks.

2. Stay Plugged into Developer Communities

Platform	Best For
Replit Forum	IDE-specific tips, Nix config, bugs
Stack Overflow	Legacy errors and fix patterns
Discord Servers	Live support for tools like LangChain, Vercel
Subreddits	Opinions, beginner-friendly explanations

🔗 Suggested: /r/LocalLLaMA, /r/learnmachinelearning, and Replit's official Discord for instant help and new feature announcements.

3. Subscribe to Curated Newsletters

Avoid being overwhelmed by noise. The best updates come from newsletters that filter and distill.

Newsletter	Focus Area
Import AI by Jack Clark	AI policy + tech strategy
The Rundown AI	Tools, launches, practical use cases
The Sequence	ML research + tutorials
Prompt Engineering Daily	Trends in generative UX
Replit Changelog	IDE and infra updates

4. Attend Virtual Events and Hackathons

Online events let you see what's being built in real time and engage directly with teams.

- **OpenAI Dev Day** (annual) – new model releases and SDKs
- **Hugging Face Spaces Demo Day** – community projects, reusable code
- **Replit Hackathons** – themed challenges (e.g., AI tools, education apps)

Replit events often include Repl templates and sponsor credits to get started quickly.

5. Experiment with New APIs

Learning by doing is still the best teacher.

- Try new models on **Hugging Face Spaces** or **OpenRouter.ai**
- Use Replit's **Secrets Manager** to switch between keys and model backends
- Build a model-explorer.py script to test generation, embeddings, or image-to-text from different APIs

```
# Example: switching between OpenAI and Mistral

if os.getenv("MODEL_BACKEND") == "openai":

    # call OpenAI API

else:

    # call local or Hugging Face model
```

6. Join Open Source AI Projects

Contributing to tools like LangChain, Haystack, or FastAPI exposes you to real-world best practices and infrastructure patterns.

- Look for "good first issue" tags on GitHub
- Try running the test suite of a repo on Replit
- Fork and tweak AI prompt templates for your own projects

7. Build and Document Your Own AI Stack

Nothing helps you internalize new AI capabilities better than teaching them to others.

- Create a public Repl with your favorite AI stack

- Write a blog post on **Dev.to, Hashnode**, or **Replit Bounties**
- Build a personal changelog of what models/tools you've used and how

Staying current with AI is not about reading everything - it's about finding reliable sources, joining the right conversations, and trying new tools with a purpose.

Further Learning Resources

Mastering AI web development is not a final destination but the beginning of a dynamic journey. The pace of advancement in AI and web technologies means that staying updated is not optional - it is essential.

1. Documentation and Official Guides

One of the most valuable habits you can develop is reading and referencing official documentation. These sources are authoritative, regularly updated, and often provide the first look at new features.

- **Replit Documentation**: Learn about the latest updates in the Replit platform, including AI features like Ghostwriter, extensions, and deployment workflows. https://docs.replit.com
- **Next.js Documentation**: For those extending their Replit apps with full-stack capabilities, Next.js is a logical step. https://nextjs.org/docs
- **OpenAI API Docs**: Since many AI-powered web apps use OpenAI's models, staying current with its capabilities is crucial. https://platform.openai.com/docs
- **Hugging Face Transformers**: For developers venturing beyond OpenAI, Hugging Face offers an ecosystem of

models and tools for advanced NLP.
https://huggingface.co/docs

2. Online Courses and Certifications

Structured learning can accelerate your understanding, especially as you dive into more complex topics like multi-model AI, edge deployment, and ethical AI design.

- **DeepLearning.AI – Generative AI Courses**
  Ideal for deepening your understanding of LLMs and their practical integration into web apps.
  https://www.deeplearning.ai

- **Coursera and edX AI Programs**
  Topics range from machine learning fundamentals to advanced deployment strategies. Institutions like Stanford, MIT, and Google Cloud offer high-quality content.

- **Replit Learn and 100 Days of Code**
  Replit's own learning portal and community challenges can reinforce skills through repetition and hands-on projects.
  https://replit.com/learn

3. GitHub Projects and Open Source Exploration

Studying open-source projects provides real-world context. Examine codebases to see how experienced developers structure AI-powered apps.

- Search GitHub for projects using tags like #AI, #Replit, #LLM, or #WebAI.

- Contribute to open issues or participate in community forks.

4. Communities and Discussion Forums

Communities can be the fastest path to solutions and insights. Whether you're debugging an issue or brainstorming app ideas, interacting with others helps expand your perspective.

- **Replit Ask**: A Q&A platform tailored to the Replit ecosystem.
  https://ask.replit.com
- **Stack Overflow**: Use for broader programming and debugging help. Tag your questions appropriately (e.g., #replit, #ai, #openai-api).
- **Discord & Reddit**: Join Replit's official Discord or subreddits like r/MachineLearning or r/Replit.

5. Blogs and Newsletters

Staying current requires reading thought pieces and news from reliable sources.

- **The Batch by Andrew Ng** - Weekly summaries of impactful AI developments.
- **Replit Changelog** – Details new Replit features and product updates.
- **Import AI by Jack Clark** – Tracks frontier AI research and its broader implications.

6. Books and Academic Papers

For those who want to dive into foundational theory or state-of-the-art research:

- *Artificial Intelligence: A Modern Approach* by Russell and Norvig -- A comprehensive textbook covering classical and modern AI.

- *Designing Machine Learning Systems* by Chip Huyen - Practical strategies for building and deploying ML systems.
- arXiv.org - A free repository of scientific papers. Use it to find the latest research on LLMs, prompt engineering, and AI ethics.

7. Your Personal AI Developer Toolkit

Create a habit of maintaining your own toolkit, such as:

- A **project repo** of AI components you've built (e.g., chatbots, summarizers, AI image generators).
- A **knowledge base** using tools like Notion or Obsidian to capture what you've learned.
- A **reading queue** of papers and blog posts.

📘 Suggested Image for This Section

Title: *"The Continuous Learning Loop for AI Web Developers"*
Visual Elements:

- Circular flow diagram
- Nodes: *Learn* → *Build* → *Share* → *Reflect* → *Update* → *Learn*
- External icons or logos: Replit, OpenAI, GitHub, YouTube, Stack Overflow
- Centerpiece: A laptop with code + neural network visualization on screen

By following these learning pathways, you not only reinforce what you've learned but position yourself to build increasingly sophisticated, intelligent web experiences.

Advanced AI Techniques and Resources

After mastering the fundamentals of AI web development on Replit - such as integrating APIs, building basic LLM applications, and deploying interactive tools - you're ready to explore more advanced AI techniques. These next steps allow you to move from integrating off-the-shelf models to fine-tuning, customizing, and deploying sophisticated AI systems with real-world impact.

1. Prompt Engineering at Scale

Prompt engineering is no longer just about clever phrasing. Advanced prompt engineering now includes dynamic prompt construction, context windows management, and chaining model calls.

Techniques to Explore:

- **Few-shot and Zero-shot Learning**: Use examples in prompts to improve output quality.
- **Dynamic Prompt Templates**: Use conditional logic in code to modify prompts based on input context.

- **ReAct and Chain-of-Thought Prompting**: Guide the model to reason step-by-step rather than generate answers directly.

Tools:

- **LangChain** and **LlamaIndex**: Frameworks for building modular prompt pipelines and agent-based systems.
- **Replit + LangChain Template Projects**: Explore Replit's templates that use LangChain for advanced use cases.

2. Model Fine-Tuning and Embedding Training

While pre-trained models like GPT-4 are powerful, sometimes they fall short in domain-specific tasks. Fine-tuning or embedding-based retrieval can drastically improve performance.

What to Learn:

- **Embedding Models**: Train models to turn documents or concepts into numerical vectors (e.g., using OpenAI embeddings or Hugging Face's sentence-transformers).
- **RAG (Retrieval-Augmented Generation)**: Combine document search and generative AI to create smarter, grounded responses.
- **Fine-Tuning with LoRA or QLoRA**: Lightweight methods to fine-tune large models efficiently using fewer compute resources.

Tools:

- **Hugging Face Transformers + Datasets**
- **Weights & Biases**: For tracking training experiments
- **Google Colab + Replit Integration**: Run fine-tuning in Colab, then deploy interfaces on Replit.

3. Multimodal AI Systems

Text-only interactions are limiting. Advanced applications increasingly incorporate **images, audio, and code** alongside natural language. These systems are called **multimodal**.

Techniques:

- **Vision + Language Models (VLMs)**: Use models like GPT-4V or CLIP to analyze or describe images.
- **Text-to-Audio and Speech Interfaces**: Integrate tools like ElevenLabs, Whisper, or Coqui TTS.
- **Multimodal Interfaces on Replit**: Build apps that combine webcam input, voice commands, and chat interfaces in a browser.

Example Use Cases:

- AI tutors that speak and read diagrams aloud
- Visual search engines
- Voice-controlled web apps

4. Agents, Tool Use, and Memory

LLMs are moving beyond static Q&A and into agentic behavior - models that make decisions, call tools, and manage memory.

Core Concepts:

- **Autonomous Agents**: Use libraries like **Auto-GPT**, **BabyAGI**, or **LangGraph** to build goal-seeking agents.
- **Tool Use and Function Calling**: Use OpenAI function calling or Replit's extensions to let the AI call APIs, databases, or perform browser actions.

- **Memory and Context Windows**: Manage long-term and short-term memory in conversation (e.g., vector databases for persistent memory).

Best Practices:

- Implement safety constraints and failover logic
- Log and monitor AI behavior with tools like **LangSmith**

5. Deployment and Edge AI

Beyond development, deploying AI apps reliably is a challenge - especially when considering cost, latency, and privacy.

Emerging Areas:

- **Edge AI**: Deploy lightweight models in the browser (e.g., with TensorFlow.js, ONNX Runtime).
- **Function-as-a-Service (FaaS)**: Use Replit Deployments, Cloudflare Workers, or Vercel Functions for scalable AI endpoints.
- **Containerization with Replit Nix**: Customize your environment for hosting AI backends with specific dependencies.

6. Ethical AI, Bias Mitigation, and Safety

Advanced AI also requires advanced responsibility. As your apps gain power, the ethical impact grows.

Topics to Explore:

- **Bias Detection and Mitigation**
- **Explainability**: How does your model reach its conclusions?
- **Data Privacy and User Consent**

- **Adversarial Prompting and Jailbreak Prevention**

Resources:

- **AI Fairness 360 Toolkit (IBM)**
- **OpenAI Safety Best Practices**
- **Partnership on AI Guidelines**

▪ Suggested Image for This Section

Title: *"Advanced AI Web Development: Technology Map"*

Visual Structure: A layered architecture map that shows increasing sophistication

Level 1: Basic APIs → GPT Chatbot → Replit UI

Level 2: Prompt Engineering → Dynamic Templates → LangChain

Level 3: RAG + Embeddings → Custom Data → Vector Stores

Level 4: Agents + Tools → Multi-Step Actions → Function Calling

Level 5: Multimodal + Edge AI → Voice, Images → TensorFlow.js

Level 6: Ethics, Safety, Privacy

Each level can be illustrated with a small icon or app snippet.

Mastering these advanced areas takes time. Choose one domain - like agents, multimodal input, or embeddings - and build a focused project around it. Let each experiment drive your curiosity. As new models and APIs emerge, stay experimental and collaborative.

Building a Career in AI Web Development

Artificial intelligence is reshaping how the web is built and experienced. Turning your project work on Replit into a sustainable career requires a deliberate strategy, consistent skill growth, and smart networking.

1. Understand the Career Landscape

Role	Primary Focus	Typical Skills	Hiring Domains
AI Web Engineer	Integrate language or vision models into full-stack apps	JavaScript/TypeScript, Python, React, model APIs, prompt design	Tech startups, product teams
AI Prototyper / Rapid Engineer	Build proof-of-concepts, hack on new model features	Replit + LangChain, UX wireframing, quick deployment	Innovation labs, agencies
ML Engineer (Web-facing)	Fine-tune and serve models behind web experiences	PyTorch, Hugging Face, vector DBs, DevOps	AI platforms, mid-size AI companies
AI Solutions Architect	Design end-to-end systems, ensure scalability and compliance	Cloud architecture, privacy, cost optimization	Enterprises, consultancies

Explore job descriptions on LinkedIn or RemoteOK to see which blend of skills is most in demand. Match gaps in your résumé to targeted learning goals.

2. Build a Business-Ready Skill Stack

1. **Core Web**: HTML, CSS, JavaScript, React or Next.js, version control.
2. **AI Integration**: Prompt engineering, OpenAI function calling, LangChain agents.
3. **Data & Storage**: Postgres, Redis, vector databases like Pinecone or Supabase Vector.
4. **DevOps**: Replit Deployments, container workflows, observability, cost monitoring.
5. **Soft Skills**: Communication, requirements gathering, concise documentation, ethical awareness.

Use Replit's Ghostwriter and Deploy features to practise end-to-end builds in a single workspace, mirroring real production flows.

3. Craft an Impactful Portfolio

- **Signature Projects**: Two or three polished demos that solve recognizable problems, e.g. a multimodal resume reviewer or a voice-controlled study assistant.
- **Code Quality**: Commit history showing tests, CI scripts, readable README files.
- **Storytelling**: Blog posts or short videos explaining design choices and AI trade-offs.
- **Live URLs**: Deploy every major project on Replit so recruiters can click and try.

Recruiters often scan portfolios in under five minutes; highlight results, not tech jargon.

4. Credentials That Matter

Credential	Why It Helps	Where to Get It
OpenAI Developer Certification *(beta)*	Demonstrates proficiency with GPT models and safety guidelines.	OpenAI
Google Professional Machine Learning Engineer	Shows understanding of production ML pipelines and reliability.	Google Cloud
Hugging Face Course Certificate	Signals hands-on experience fine-tuning and hosting models.	Hugging Face
100 Days of Replit Badge	Reflects commitment to daily coding and community participation.	Replit

Certificates do not replace skill, but they can get your résumé past automated filters.

5. Network With Intent

- **Replit Discord & Ask**: Share projects, request feedback, spot internal job postings.
- **Meetups and Hackathons**: Local AI or web dev events accelerate serendipitous hiring conversations.
- **Open-Source Contribution**: Even a merged typo fix gets your name in important repos and shows collaboration.

- **Cold Outreach**: Short, value-focused messages to hiring managers can bypass crowded job portals. Refer to a specific project of theirs and suggest how you can help.

6. Interview Preparation

1. **Technical Deep Dives**: Be ready to whiteboard a prompt-engineering workflow or explain RAG latency bottlenecks.
2. **Live Coding in Replit**: Many companies now spin up shared Replit sessions; practise solving problems there.
3. **System-Design Scenarios**: Sketch an architecture for a multilingual chat assistant that caches embeddings and scales to 10 000 concurrent users.
4. **Ethics Questions**: Prepare opinions on bias mitigation, user consent, and rate limiting.

7. Professional Growth After Landing the Job

- **Mentorship**: Request one-on-ones with senior ML or product leaders.
- **Continuous Education Budget**: Many employers fund conferences like AI-Dev or courses on DeepLearning.AI; ask early.
- **Internal Demos**: Run monthly "lunch-and-learn" sessions showcasing your experiments. Public speaking amplifies your visibility.
- **Specialize or Generalize**: Follow your curiosity - whether in multimodal systems, edge inference, or AI governance - and align it with business needs.

8. Freelancing and Entrepreneurship

If autonomy appeals to you:

- **Niche Down**: Position yourself as "the Replit + GPT-4V prototype specialist" instead of a generic full-stack dev.
- **Productize**: Convert successful client scaffolds into reusable SaaS templates.
- **Retainer Models**: Offer continuous model-tuning and cost-optimization packages.

Balancing client acquisition and delivery is challenging; track your hours and build repeatable processes early.

9. Future-Proof Mindset

- Schedule weekly reading of release notes from OpenAI, Replit, and major open-source libraries.
- Experiment with at least one new model or tool each month.
- Keep a personal changelog of what you tried, what failed, and why; reflection turns experience into expertise.

Career Pathway Illustration

Below is a visual "AI Web Development Career Pathway" you can reference in presentations or personal planning.

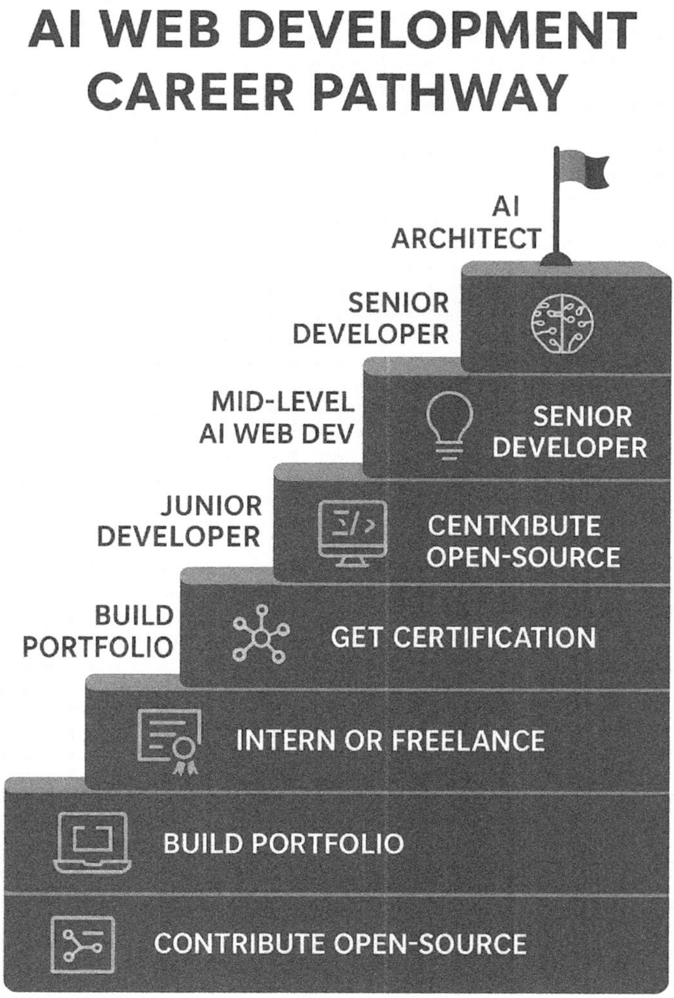
AI WEB DEVELOPMENT
CAREER PATHWAY
AI
ARCHITECT
SENIOR
DEVELOPER
MID-LEVEL
AI WEB DEV
JUNIOR
DEVELOPER
BUILD
PORTFOLIO
SENIOR
DEVELOPER
CENTKIBUTE
OPEN-SOURCE
GET CERTIFICATION
INTERN OR FREELANCE
BUILD PORTFOLIO
CONTRIBUTE OPEN-SOURCE

Appendices

Appendix A: Quick Reference Guide

Use this appendix as a compact cheat-sheet during daily development on Replit. Keep it open in a second tab or print it for your desk. It is organized by common tasks so you can find answers fast.

1. Workspace Navigation

Keyboard shortcuts (macOS / Windows-Linux)

- Command + E / Ctrl + E, Open file explorer filter.
- Command + P / Ctrl + P, Fuzzy-find any file.
- Command + Shift + P / Ctrl + Shift + P, Command palette for all actions.
- Option + Shift + F / Alt + Shift + F, Format code with Prettier or Black.
- Command + / Ctrl +, Toggle console.
- Command + B / Ctrl + B, Hide-show sidebar.

Tip: In multi-tab sessions press **Command + 1-9 / Ctrl + 1-9** to jump directly to the nth open editor tab.

2. Replit Command Palette Gems

Action	Palette command
Run current file	run
Open Secrets dialog	secrets
Fork public template	fork

Action	Palette command
Enable Nix packages	nix: search then nix: install
Deploy to URL	deploy

Enter characters in the palette to fuzzy-search. No need to type full words.

3. Project Setup Snippets

```
# Create virtual environment (Python)

python -m venv venv && source venv/bin/activate


# Install latest OpenAI SDK

pip install --upgrade openai


# Install LangChain + vector store helpers

pip install langchain[all] sentence_transformers pinecone-client

# JavaScript quick start

npm init -y

npm install openai@latest langchain dotenv
```

4. Replit AI Helpers

Feature	Usage example
Ghostwriter Explain	Highlight code, press ••• > "Explain selection"

Feature	Usage example
Ghostwriter Generate	Type comment: # create REST endpoint for /embed then press **Tab**
Conversations	Press **Esc Esc** to open chat without leaving the editor

Ghostwriter credits reset monthly on the Hacker plan, track usage in **Account → AI**.

5. Deployment Checklist

1. **Secrets**: Add keys in *Secrets* panel, not in code.
2. **Environment**: Configure *replit.nix* or *requirements.txt / package.json.*
3. **Port**: Bind to process.env.PORT (Node) or os.getenv("PORT", 3000) (Python).
4. **run.sh**: Ensure single entry script, e.g. python main.py.
5. **Deploy button**: Click **Deploy → Static / Autoscale / Reserved VM**; confirm pricing.

6. OpenAI Quick Calls

```
import openai

openai.api_key = os.getenv("OPENAI_API_KEY")


response = openai.chat.completions.create(

  model="gpt-4o-mini",

  messages=[

    {"role":"system","content":"You are a helpful assistant"},
```

```
    {"role":"user","content":"Explain RAG"}
  ]
)
print(response.choices[0].message.content)
import OpenAI from "openai";
const openai = new OpenAI();

const res = await openai.chat.completions.create({
  model: "gpt-4o-mini",
  messages: [
    {role: "system", content: "You are a helpful assistant"},
    {role: "user", content: "Give me a prompt-engineering tip"}
  ]
});
console.log(res.choices[0].message.content);
```

7. Debugging at Speed

- **Console logs**: Use console.table() or pprint() for structured objects.
- **Hot reload**: In Node add npm install nodemon --save-dev, run nodemon index.js.
- **Breakpoints**: Click gutter or use debugger statement then press **Run → Debug**.

8. Common Error Fixes

Symptom	Likely cause	Quick fix
App hangs on "Listening on 0.0.0.0"	Wrong port	Bind to env PORT variable
ModuleNotFoundError after install	Incompatible pip cache	pip install--no-cache-dir package
OpenAI 429 errors	Rate limit	Add time.sleep, reduce request frequency
"EADDRINUSE" on restart	Dev server still alive	Stop run or kill process from Shell

9. One-Line Utilities

```
# Watch .py and restart
while inotifywait -e modify *.py; do python main.py; done
// Measure token count with tiktoken
npx @dqbd/tiktoken-cli "Your prompt text here"
```

10. Further Help Fast

Resource	URL
Replit Docs	docs.replit.com
Replit Ask (community Q&A)	ask.replit.com

Resource	URL
OpenAI Cookbook	github.com/openai/openai-cookbook
LangChain Hub	smith.langchain.com/hub

Appendix B: Resources and Links

This appendix offers a curated collection of the most useful resources for AI web development on Replit. Whether you are looking to deepen your technical skills, troubleshoot an issue, stay informed about the latest tools, or expand your network, the links below will serve as a reliable launchpad.

🔧 Official Documentation and Tools

Resource	Description	Link
Replit Docs	Comprehensive guide to using the Replit IDE, deployments, templates, secrets management, and extensions.	https://docs.replit.com
OpenAI API Documentation	Explains how to integrate GPT, Whisper, and DALL·E models via API, with code examples in multiple languages.	https://platform.openai.com/docs

Resource	Description	Link
LangChain Documentation	Toolkits and guides for creating agents, RAG apps, and prompt workflows using language models.	https://docs.langchain.com
Hugging Face Hub	Host and explore thousands of pre-trained AI models and datasets, with support for Transformers, Diffusers, and more.	https://huggingface.co/models
Supabase Docs	If you're using a database in your AI apps, Supabase offers an open-source Postgres-based backend with vector support.	https://supabase.com/docs

---

🧠 Learning Platforms and Courses

Platform	Highlights	Link
Replit Learn	Interactive coding challenges and tutorials. Includes AI and web	https://replit.com/learn

Platform	Highlights	Link
	development tracks.	
DeepLearning.AI	Professional AI courses including Generative AI with LangChain and Prompt Engineering for Developers.	https://www.deeplearning.ai
Fast.ai	Practical deep learning course built for coders. Excellent for diving into model training later in your journey.	https://course.fast.ai
Coursera & edX AI Specializations	Structured AI and ML curricula by Stanford, Google, and MIT.	https://coursera.org, https://edx.org
Hugging Face Course	A hands-on guide to NLP and model deployment.	https://huggingface.co/learn/nlp-course

🛠 Developer Tools and Libraries

Tool	Purpose	Link
Tiktoken	Tokenizer used to count tokens for OpenAI models. Helps manage costs and context windows.	https://github.com/openai/tiktoken
LangSmith	Track, evaluate, and debug LLM applications built with LangChain.	https://smith.langchain.com
Whisper	OpenAI's automatic speech recognition system, usable via CLI or Python.	https://github.com/openai/whisper
Replicate	Run AI models from the command line or web; ideal for ML models outside of OpenAI's ecosystem.	https://replicate.com

Tool	Purpose	Link
Vector Stores	Pinecone, Weaviate, and Chroma provide embeddings search for AI apps.	
Replit Extensions	Add features like Postgres, vector search, or analytics directly into your workspace.	https://replit.com/extensions

Communities and Forums

Community	Description	Link
Replit Ask	Replit's official Q&A forum. Great for getting help from fellow developers.	https://ask.replit.com
Replit Discord	Join thousands of Replit users sharing tips, debugging help, and project showcases.	https://replit.com/discord
Stack Overflow	Use tags like #replit, #openai, #langchain,	https://stackoverflow.com

Community	Description	Link
	and #webdev for technical questions.	
Hugging Face Forum	Engage with model developers and contributors for help or feedback.	https://discuss.huggingface.co
GitHub Discussions	Follow issue threads and community conversations on the open-source tools you use.	https://github.com

📬 Newsletters and Blogs

Source	Why Subscribe	Link
The Batch (by DeepLearning.AI)	Weekly digest of major AI developments, model releases, and tools.	https://www.deeplearning.ai/the-batch/
Import AI (by Jack Clark)	Insightful commentary on global AI trends, policy, and research.	https://jack-clark.net

Source	Why Subscribe	Link
Replit Changelog	Official Replit feature updates, bug fixes, and new tools.	https://replit.com/changelog
Hacker News AI tag	Get raw community perspectives and links to technical deep-dives.	https://news.ycombinator.com

Templates and Starter Projects

Resource	Description	Link
Replit AI Templates	Ready-to-fork projects for chatbots, summarizers, and more. Great for learning by doing.	https://replit.com/@replit/ai
LangChain Templates on GitHub	Sample projects for agents, Q&A apps, document loaders, and chains.	https://github.com/langchain-ai/langchain

Resource	Description	Link
OpenAI Cookbook	Recipes and guides on working with GPT, DALL·E, function calling, embeddings, and Whisper.	https://github.com/openai/openai-cookbook
AI Web App Examples	Search GitHub for #gpt-webapp, #replit, #langchain-agent, etc. to see real code.	https://github.com

Appendix C: Glossary of Terms

This glossary provides clear, concise definitions of the most important terms and acronyms you'll encounter while building AI-powered web applications using Replit.

A

- **API (Application Programming Interface)**
  A standardized way for programs to talk to each other. In AI web development, APIs like OpenAI or Hugging Face allow apps to access powerful AI models via HTTP requests.
- **Agent**
  An AI process or application that performs autonomous or semi-autonomous tasks, often by making decisions and calling tools or functions. Common in frameworks like LangChain.

- **Autoscale Deployment (Replit)**
  A Replit deployment mode where your application is automatically scaled up or down based on demand, reducing idle costs and handling traffic spikes.

B

- **Backend**
  The server-side logic of a web app, responsible for tasks like processing data, handling APIs, and managing databases.
- **Bias (AI)**
  Systematic errors in model outputs due to skewed training data or flawed assumptions, which can affect fairness and safety.

C

- **Chat Completion**
  An OpenAI endpoint used to power chat-like interactions between a user and a model. Accepts system, user, and assistant messages as input.
- **Command Palette**
  A Replit feature (opened with Ctrl+Shift+P or Cmd+Shift+P) that lets you run IDE commands quickly via text.
- **Context Window**
  The maximum number of tokens (words or subwords) a language model can "remember" or process in a single input-output session.

D

- **Deployment**
  Publishing your app to a live environment. In Replit, you can deploy using Static, Autoscale, or Reserved VM modes.
- **Dynamic Prompting**
  Generating or modifying prompts in real time, based on user input, system state, or application logic.

E

- **Embedding**
  A numerical vector representation of text, images, or other data. Commonly used for search, semantic similarity, and retrieval-augmented generation (RAG).
- **Environment Variables**
  Key-value pairs used to securely store configuration data like API keys. Managed through Replit's *Secrets* panel.

F

- **Frontend**
  The client-facing portion of a web application that users interact with, built using HTML, CSS, and JavaScript frameworks like React.
- **Function Calling (OpenAI)**
  A mechanism that lets a language model call external functions by returning structured data, often used for tool use or task automation.

G

- **Ghostwriter**
  Replit's built-in AI coding assistant that helps with autocompletion, code explanation, generation, and debugging.

- **GPU (Graphics Processing Unit)**
  A type of processor used to accelerate machine learning model training and inference, especially for large-scale computations.

H

- **Hosting**
  Making your web application accessible via the internet. Replit includes built-in hosting with automatic HTTPS support.

I

- **Inference**
  The process of running a trained AI model on new data to produce an output (e.g., generating text, classifying images).

- **IDE (Integrated Development Environment)**
  A software suite that combines tools like a code editor, debugger, and terminal. Replit is a cloud-based IDE.

J

- **JSON (JavaScript Object Notation)**
  A lightweight data format used to exchange information

between frontends, backends, and APIs. Often used in API responses.

L

- **LangChain**
  A framework for building applications that use large language models in pipelines or agent-like systems, often with memory and tool integration.
- **LLM (Large Language Model)**
  A neural network trained on vast text corpora to generate human-like language. Examples include GPT-4, Claude, and LLaMA.

M

- **Modal (UI)**
  A pop-up interface element that temporarily interrupts the main interface, often used for confirmations or settings.
- **Multimodal**
  AI models or applications that can handle more than one type of input, such as combining text, images, and audio.

N

- **Natural Language Processing (NLP)**
  The field of AI that focuses on teaching computers to understand, interpret, and generate human language.
- **Nix**
  The configuration language used in Replit to manage

development environments and dependencies for your workspace.

O

- **OpenAI**
  An AI research and deployment company that provides APIs for LLMs, image generation, speech-to-text, and more. Creator of GPT models.

P

- **Prompt**
  The text or data you provide to an AI model to instruct it to perform a task. Prompt design is a key part of working effectively with LLMs.
- **Prompt Engineering**
  The practice of crafting prompts that produce desired outcomes from a language model. Often involves iteration, testing, and fine-tuning.

R

- **RAG (Retrieval-Augmented Generation)**
  A technique that enhances LLM outputs by retrieving relevant external documents and feeding them into the prompt.
- **Reserved VM (Replit)**
  A deployment tier that gives your app a dedicated virtual machine for predictable performance and uptime.

S

- **Secrets (Replit)**
  Replit's environment variable manager used to store API keys, passwords, and configuration values securely.
- **State Management**
  The process of handling data changes in frontend applications, often using tools like Redux, Zustand, or React's Context API.

T

- **Token**
  A chunk of text (word, subword, or character) used in LLM processing. Token limits constrain input and output length.
- **Transformer**
  A type of neural network architecture that powers most modern LLMs. Known for its attention mechanism.

U

- **UI (User Interface)**
  The visual part of your application that users see and interact with.
- **UX (User Experience)**
  The overall experience a user has while interacting with an app, shaped by design, performance, and usability.

V

- **Vector Database**
  A special type of database designed to store and search embeddings efficiently. Used in semantic search and RAG workflows.

W

- **Webhooks**
  HTTP callbacks triggered by external events, often used to integrate APIs and automate workflows.
- **WebSocket**
  A communication protocol that enables real-time, two-way data exchange between a client and a server.

Y

- **YAML**
  A human-readable configuration format used in Nix and other system files.

Appendix D: Replit and AI Cheat Sheets

This appendix compiles high-utility cheat sheets covering common commands, code snippets, workflows, and patterns specific to Replit and AI integration. Use these reference guides to accelerate development, avoid repetitive troubleshooting, and stay productive when working on intelligent web apps.

🚀 Replit Development Cheat Sheet

Common Replit Commands

Action	Shortcut / Command
Open Command Palette	Ctrl + Shift + P / Cmd + Shift + P
Run current file	Ctrl + Enter or click **Run**
Toggle console	`Ctrl + ``
Format code	Alt + Shift + F / Option + Shift + F
Rename file	Right-click > Rename or F2
Deploy project	Click **Deploy** → choose method

Replit Secrets (Environment Variables)

Add securely from UI:

Secrets tab → Key: OPENAI_API_KEY → Value: your-key

Access in code:

```
import os

api_key = os.getenv("OPENAI_API_KEY")

const apiKey = process.env.OPENAI_API_KEY;
```

📦 Package Installation Cheat Sheet

Python

```
# Common installs

pip install openai langchain python-dotenv

pip install tiktoken sentence-transformers chromadb
```

JavaScript / Node.js

```
npm install openai langchain dotenv express
```

OpenAI API Cheat Sheet

Chat Completion (Python)

```
import openai


openai.api_key = os.getenv("OPENAI_API_KEY")


response = openai.chat.completions.create(
    model="gpt-4o",
    messages=[
        {"role": "system", "content": "You are a helpful assistant."},
        {"role": "user", "content": "What is retrieval-augmented
generation?"}
    ]
)


print(response.choices[0].message.content)
```

Chat Completion (JavaScript)

```
import OpenAI from "openai";


const openai = new OpenAI({ apiKey:
process.env.OPENAI_API_KEY });
```

```
const res = await openai.chat.completions.create({
  model: "gpt-4o",
  messages: [
    { role: "system", content: "You are a helpful assistant." },
    { role: "user", content: "Explain prompt engineering." }
  ]
});

console.log(res.choices[0].message.content);
```

Function Calling (Python)

```
functions = [
    {
        "name": "get_weather",
        "description": "Gets the weather for a location",
        "parameters": {
            "type": "object",
            "properties": {
                "location": {"type": "string"}
            },
            "required": ["location"]
        }
```

```
    }
]

response = openai.chat.completions.create(
    model="gpt-4o",
    messages=[
        {"role": "user", "content": "What's the weather in Paris?"}
    ],
    functions=functions,
    function_call="auto"
)
```

🔗 LangChain Quick Reference

```
from langchain.chat_models import ChatOpenAI
from langchain.prompts import ChatPromptTemplate
from langchain.chains import LLMChain

llm = ChatOpenAI(model="gpt-4", temperature=0.7)

prompt = ChatPromptTemplate.from_template(
    "Translate the following English to French: {input}"
)
```

```
chain = LLMChain(llm=llm, prompt=prompt)


response = chain.run(input="Hello, how are you?")
print(response)
```

🧰 Prompt Engineering Patterns

Pattern	Example
Few-shot prompting	Provide 2-3 examples before asking the AI to continue.
Chain-of-thought	Add "Let's think step-by-step..." to guide reasoning.
ReAct pattern	Combine reasoning + actions (used in agent design).
Instructional	"You are an expert Python tutor. Explain recursion."

📊 Token Management

Python: Count tokens using tiktoken

```
import tiktoken


enc = tiktoken.encoding_for_model("gpt-4")
tokens = enc.encode("Translate this sentence.")
print(f"Token count: {len(tokens)}")
```

Tips:

- GPT-4: ~8192–128k tokens (varies by model version).
- 1 token ≈ 0.75 words.

🛠 Troubleshooting Fast Fixes

Problem	Fix
Server won't start	Ensure port is bound: os.getenv("PORT", 3000) or process.env.PORT
Model returns 429	Rate limited - retry with exponential backoff
Code not deploying	Check run.sh, use correct entry file
Secrets not loading	Re-enter in Replit Secrets tab; restart the repl
CORS error	For browser fetches, add correct headers on server

Deployment Flow (Replit)

1. Test app using **Run**.
2. Add secrets and env variables.
3. Check ports and logs.
4. Click **Deploy** → Choose **Autoscale** or **Reserved VM**.
5. Monitor deployment status and public URL.

🎯 Best Practices Cheat Sheet

Area	Practice
Prompting	Iterate with prompt templates and examples.
Security	Never expose keys in source code or frontend.
Efficiency	Reuse embeddings and cache AI outputs.
Scalability	Use autoscale only when needed; monitor token usage.
Debugging	Use console.log(), print(), and terminal output for tracing.

www.ingramcontent.com/pod-product-compliance
Ingram Content Group UK Ltd.
Pitfield, Milton Keynes, MK11 3LW, UK
UKHW020127290926
15471UKWH00003B/333

9 798349 472